Learning to Lead

Learning to LEAD

Second edition

Effective
Leadership Skills
for Teachers of Young Children

Debra Ren-Etta Sullivan

Redleaf Press®
www.redleafpress.org
800-423-8309

Published by Redleaf Press
10 Yorkton Court
St. Paul, MN 55117
www.redleafpress.org

Second edition 2010
Interior typeset in Baskerville
Printed in the United States of America
20 19 18 17 16 15 14 13   4 5 6 7 8 9 10 11

Library of Congress Cataloging-in-Publication Data
Sullivan, Debra Ren-Etta.
    Learning to lead : effective leadership skills for teachers of young children /
Debra Ren-Etta Sullivan.—2nd ed.
        p. cm.
    Includes bibliographical references and index.
    ISBN 978-1-60554-018-4 (alk. paper)
    1. Early childhood education—Administration. 2. Educational leadership.
I. Title.
LB2822.6.S85 2010
372.11—dc22
                                2009026313

Printed on acid-free paper

I dedicate this book to every child, in loving memory of
Dr. Zakiya Mawanatabu Stewart. Mother Zakiya dedicated her life the
most to children who had the least. Every child has a right to an
excellent education. Our best teaching and our best
leadership will guarantee that right.

I also dedicate this book to my beloved son, Aaron John Sullivan.

Contents

Preface

▲

I have often been asked why I decided to write this book. There are numerous books out there on leadership, books for almost any field imaginable. For many years, I have taught undergraduate and graduate leadership classes to students preparing for early childhood and elementary education. I have worked with preschool, kindergarten, and elementary teachers negotiating changes in student demographics, curriculum, building-level leadership, and staffing. I have presented conference workshops that bring together care providers, teachers, parents, and social-service workers to collaborate on moving away from what others should be doing and toward what each individual can do to improve the service, care, and education of children.

In all of these situations, I often come across the same two problems. First, many of the students in my classes see true leadership as something that belongs to great people, not as something they can achieve themselves. Students often experience a moment of surprise when they realize we are not going to talk about people like Barack Obama, Mother Teresa, José Rizal, or Docia Zavitkovsky, but instead are going to examine their own roles in the leadership process.

Second, although early childhood educators continue to struggle with the challenges of being overlooked when it comes to the leadership potential, qualities, and abilities of those who care for and teach children, very little leadership literature is written for child care professionals who work directly with children. Yet, these are people who share in the leadership process every day, spotting problems and working toward solutions. These are the teachers, care providers, aides, and assistants who have direct responsibility for the care and education of young children.

While leadership applies to everyone connected with the field of early childhood care and education, this book is addressed to the people who constitute the majority of early care and education workers: teachers. They are people like you, who have been and will continue to be part of the leadership process.

This book is about your personal development as a teacher and a leader. If you work with children, you are a teacher. Even if you are just standing in a room with children, you are a teacher. Children learn. That's all they do. It's their job. They learn from what you do and what you don't do. They learn from what you say and what you don't say. They learn from what you allow and what you won't allow. They learn from what you act on and what you don't act on. They learn from what you notice and what you don't notice. Children learn from you how to treat people and what to expect of others. If children are present, they are learning. If you are present with them, you are teaching. It is for this reason that the term *teacher* is used here to include all teachers, child care providers, aides, assistants, program/activity coordinators, and other staff, such as the cook, who work in early care and education settings.

Leadership is similar to teaching. If you are interacting with other people, you are leading. How you behave with other people has an effect on what they think they can do, how they approach problems, and what they will consider. If other people are present, they are responding to you. They notice how you hold your body and if you look tired or bored or interested or enthusiastic or angry. They hear how you react to questions, to problems, to changes, to good news. If you work in a child care center, school, or similar organization, everything you do or don't do contributes to the way the organization functions. This is leadership.

Every adult needs to acknowledge, be responsible, and be accountable for the impact she has on the life of a child. Children look to us for learning, and we provide it, whether we intend to or not. In the same way, you are leading whether you intend to or not, whether you are the director of the child care center, a home provider at a licensing meeting, or the infant-room teacher. That's why it's so important to acknowledge your leadership—are you leading others in the direction you want to go?

Teaching and leading have other similarities. They involve many of the same skills. Because you are a good teacher, you can be a good leader as well. You are already doing it. You already know how. It's just a matter of recognizing your leadership and paying attention. You do this with children every day. You can do it with adults too.

This book is designed to give you an introduction to leadership theory and practice whether you work in a center, family child care setting, preschool, school-age care setting, or any other work environment involving children. You'll learn the definitions of what leadership is (and is not) and some functions and styles of leadership. You'll learn about the roles of empowerment, followership, and advocacy in leadership, as well as your own role in facilitating the development of leadership in others. You'll learn how to use your knowledge of child development to understand leadership development and how to transfer your natural skills and abilities to a number of leadership situations and circumstances. Being able to transfer your abilities from one area to another will help you recognize the leader within.

Each chapter is built around a combination of theories, examples, and reflection questions—all designed to give you opportunities to fully examine and fully appreciate your own strengths, gifts, attitudes, values, challenges, and motivations and reflect on how these influence your leadership development. And what good is a book if it doesn't contain some stories? Each chapter ends with a little vignette that puts some of the ideas you've read into action. It is not possible to include everything you need to know about leadership in one book, so I have also included ideas, information, and references for further study, learning, and practice.

While playing with blocks, children learn about weight, balance, gravity, construction, destruction, addition, subtraction, and working with other children. In much the same way that children transfer playing to learning possibilities, I hope you will transfer the knowledge you gain from reading this book to your everyday life. Using this book, you will examine your ability to change the world. To the young child, all adults are leaders and have the power, authority, and status to change the world. Just turn the page to begin understanding and implementing what young children already know!

Acknowledgments

I have loved working with the Redleaf Press team! I still give many thanks to my first editor, Beth Wallace. With even more thanks and with much appreciation, I can add my latest editor, Kyra Ostendorf, and Redleaf's editor-in-chief, David Heath, for their wonderful patience in and zest for what this book could be. In the first edition, I gave a very special thank you to my friends and colleagues at Pacific Oaks College Northwest and the Early Childhood Equity Alliance for helping me see the many faces of leadership and the many gifts we bring to the leadership process. Many of them joined me in the creation and development of the Praxis Institute for Early Childhood Education, where we continue our collaborative work on behalf of the children and families who need our leadership the most. The newest members of our team (see *) have added much to the strength of our work together. Thank you!

Veronica Barrera
Sharon Cronin
Fran Davidson
Louise Derman-Sparks
Kimberly Early *
Jodi Golden-White *
Wendy Harris
Cynthia Holloway

Charlotte Jahn *
Theressa Lenear
Wei Li-Chen
Faye Louie
Mehret Mehanzel
Leticia Nieto
John Nimmo
Dale Otto *

Diana Puente
Merrilee Runyan
Joan Shelby
Tilman Smith
Zakiya Stewart
Susan Talaro
Lori Yonemitsu

Chapter 1

▲

Leadership in Early Childhood Education

In this chapter, I will discuss various ways of looking at leaders and leadership. You will have an opportunity to think about leadership's developmental nature, the way the leadership process is mutually influenced by leaders and followers, and the many roles and words used to describe leaders. You will learn the differences between leadership, power, authority, and status. You will explore the relationship between leadership development and human development. Finally, you will have an opportunity to think about what leadership means to you. But first, let's take a look at why we need leadership in our field and at the challenges and obstacles we face because our profession is composed almost entirely of women working with children.

Why Do We Need Leaders and Leadership in Early Childhood Care and Education?

There are 2.3 million people serving approximately 12 million children under the age of 6 every day. Another 3 million children participate in after-school and summer programs and many millions more are in public or private primary grades. For each child, you and your colleagues serve as important teachers. Each and every one of your words, actions, reactions, values, beliefs, interests, priorities, and perspectives (and a host of other things) provide the children with a model of what kind of person they can

1

become and what they should learn about their world. Such a big responsibility requires leadership from many people. For the children in our classrooms, we look for teaching that is intellectually and creatively stimulating, developmentally and culturally appropriate for the children being served, and socially responsive to the needs of families and communities. Outside of the classroom, we look for curricular and organizational leadership from teachers. From directors and managers, we seek guidance and vision in staff trainings, the management of resources, the setting of goals and outcomes, and the establishment of good relationships with families and outside agencies. We seek political leadership in advocates who can give voice to such issues as worthy wages, clear and accessible career paths, and the impact of quality child care on our children's futures. From our neighborhoods and communities, we hear the call for leaders in early care and education who can address the needs and realities of families, form collaborative relationships for social change, and recognize the essential role of families and communities in raising children successfully.

Leadership through collaboration, cooperation, and communication on all our parts will improve and strengthen the whole system. Employees and advocates in the field may think of early childhood care and education (ECE) as a series of discrete environments and institutions serving children of a limited age range, but to children and families, it is one continuous process that builds on previous experiences. If leadership in ECE is truly to affect our children and families in beneficial ways, we must begin to view it from their perspectives. Seeing the educational system as a single entity can increase collaboration and cooperation among family child care settings, centers, school-age care settings, preschools, and elementary schools.

As a parent or a professional, you may find yourself involved in many child-related contexts throughout your life. For example, your work in community collaboration as a school-age care provider may become critical when you act as an advocate in a family-services campaign. As a family child care provider, your close, collaborative efforts with families may become the key ingredient in planning family involvement at a child care center. Your firsthand experiences with children's developmental stages in your work at a child care center may influence your parenting style at home. In all of these examples, your ability to understand the impact of leadership on children and their families can help change society and the future of early childhood care and education in ways you can't begin to imagine!

Obstacles to Early Childhood Leadership

Many obstacles to leadership occur in early childhood care and education. Our field is almost entirely composed of women drawn to a nurturing environment, working with young children, participating in the growth of others, and putting the needs of others above their own. This makes developing leaders difficult, given that leadership development is self-focused, often rigorous or conflictual, and involves teachers in situations and activities that may feel uncomfortable.

In addition, our field is often undervalued. Our pay is low, our benefits are minimal or nonexistent, our turnover is high, there are few entry requirements and even fewer opportunities for our professional development or training, and our pathways for career advancement are unclear. We have yet to develop an inclusive definition of leadership that takes into account its need at all levels and in all areas. In many cases, we are not even sure how we really feel about leadership. Because of this, we compete with each other—level against level, setting against setting, public against private—for the few resources that are available.

We can be sure that if we are ambivalent about the need for and definition of leadership within our field, those on the outside looking in at us are even more confused. Developing future leaders in such an environment is incredibly difficult! Some critics have suggested that we hesitate to provide rewards and incentives for leadership development because those of us with more skills may be drawn to positions outside the classroom. We can't have it both ways. If we need leaders in our profession, we must be willing to help develop and reward them. We must acknowledge existing leadership at all levels of the profession, formally and informally.

What Is Leadership?

What is leadership and who are leaders? Leadership means different things to different people and is defined differently in different settings and environments. Nevertheless, at least two common factors are evident in most definitions of leaders and leadership:

- Leadership is a group phenomenon. At least two people must be involved—a leader must be leading someone.

- Leadership usually involves intentional influence. At least one of the people involved must want to make something happen.

A few more things are known about leadership. The development of leadership ability takes time. It is a lifelong process that begins at birth and is influenced by many factors, including life and work experiences. Operating the most sought-after family child care center in your community, for example, didn't just happen in a day. When you first started, you may not have had all the knowledge, information, and experience you needed. However, if you got along well with younger children when you were a child, raised a number of children of your own, took a few classes in child development, or worked in a center for a while, you began to pull together experiences that led you toward your goal. You learned different things from each experience, and you put them all together in a way that made sense to you. This process of integrating your experience gave you what you needed to begin your own family child care business. It made you a leader. And with more experiences, development, and learning comes a lot more leadership development!

Self-sufficiency and Interdependence

Effective leadership encourages a person's or a group's growth in self-sufficiency and interdependence. We foster self-sufficiency when we work to make sure that everyone has an opportunity to contribute to the leadership process—growing into our own leadership potential and assisting others in growing into theirs. Effective leadership creates interdependence: we find ways to work together and draw on each other's unique gifts and strengths so we can accomplish common goals and achieve great things.

Take, for example, a new director who has just begun working in a child care center. She has a great vision for the future of the center and really wants teachers to participate more in decisions that affect the center's overall work environment. Unfortunately, she also has a difficult time getting them to buy in to some of her ideas. The lead teacher, on the other hand, does not have a lot of information about participatory decisions, but she really knows how to communicate with other teachers and has an uncanny knack for guessing exactly how each of them will respond in a particular situation. By working together and sharing an interdependence, the director and the lead teacher can combine their skills to meet all needs. By collaborating, the director and the lead teacher develop new leadership skills. The director learns how to incorporate more ideas from others in her planning, and the lead teacher learns more about participatory decision making. In this process, each becomes more self-sufficient.

MUTUAL INFLUENCE

Leadership includes the recognition of individual strengths, contributions, and responsibilities. It is a subtle process of leaders and followers influencing each other. This process combines thoughts, beliefs, values, perspectives, expectations, feelings, and actions. It makes it possible for leaders and followers to collectively achieve purposes and values they both share.

In your work with children, you can see how teachers and children constantly influence each other. Everything you do is modeled and transferred to young children, who learn by modeling and mimicking the adults around them. At the same time, children also have their own set of thoughts, beliefs, values, perspectives, expectations, feelings, and actions. When children teach you what they want to happen in their learning environment, you make adjustments so you can better meet their needs and hold their interest.

The process is similar for leaders and followers. Both followers and leaders have their own sets of thoughts, beliefs, values, and dreams. A leader's actions are a model for those who follow him, and followers are always learning from the leader. At the same time, a good leader is also learning what others in the group want to have happen in the organization or on the project and how they want it to happen. He uses this information to change policies, revise the goals of the project, and rethink how he is leading.

Who Are Leaders?

Leaders are individuals who influence others in a way that encourages them to higher or better performance and personal development. Effective leaders may or may not have authority, position, or status. They do, however, have integrity, dignity, and respect for others. Leaders empower, encourage, and support others in a shared effort to achieve goals or create change. Leaders can be found at all levels and in a variety of positions in early childhood care and education. They take action where action is needed, and they enable others to take action when their strengths and abilities are needed. Effective leaders care about other people. They see their relationship to and with others as essential to the overall strength and vitality of the group or organization. Effective leaders and effective leadership generate more leaders, thereby strengthening the leadership process itself.

Early childhood teachers are familiar with providing encouraging, empowering, and supportive learning environments for children so each and every child has opportunities to learn. In this way we strengthen the learning process. We can also provide this kind of learning environment for each other by encouraging better performance and personal development from each other. Veteran teachers can take newcomers under their wings and point out areas for growing and learning. This process is best implemented with respect for the new teacher who is learning to master a new task and is still developing, not unlike the way a teacher helps a child who is learning to master a new task. Just like the child, the new teacher has the potential to master that task and teach it to someone else. In this way we add to the leadership pool and the leadership process.

How you see your role will influence what kind of leadership you bring to a situation. For example, leaders have been described as scouts—those who go out ahead of the rest to show the way. Other terms used to describe leaders are *architect, catalyst, advocate, prophet, mediator,* and *coach*. Leaders might be considered poets who look at their work settings from a variety of perspectives. Leaders can be designers and stewards who build communities in which people continually expand their capabilities. Leaders are learners, performers, power brokers, and role models. All of these terms describe leaders who play primary roles in making an organization or group better for its members. How you define your own role as a leader also provides many clues to how you perceive your relationship with children and their families.

Keep in mind the cultural values that influence your conception of a leader's role. In many African and African American communities, for example, great leaders have the twin roles of spokesperson, voicing the concerns of the community, and follower, being directed from the community for which she claims to speak. In the early childhood field, these twin roles of spokesperson and follower can be found in the political advocate who is an excellent spokesperson because she has been a teacher and understands the needs and challenges of the profession. Nevertheless, to be an effective leader, she must also continue to be perceived as a member of the teaching community—the teachers for whom she advocates must see her as one of their own—someone who follows their lead and perspective. This is particularly true in the African and African American early childhood community, but it is important in any leadership setting.

ASK YOURSELF

Does one of the terms used to describe leaders ring true for you and the way you see your role in your work setting? How does that role influence your relationship with the children and their families? For example, what does your work mean for children and families if you see yourself as an architect? What are you building? How will you build it? How will you know if what you are building meets the needs of the children and families you serve?

In what ways does your leadership provide others with opportunities to perform better and develop personally?

How do you know you are providing an encouraging, empowering, and supportive environment? What characteristics would you look for in this kind of environment?

In what ways are the children you teach likely to become teachers of their peers? In what ways are the teachers you lead likely to become leaders of their peers?

In what ways do the least privileged children and teachers in your group benefit from your leadership? Think about the children in your classroom who have the fewest resources, such as family, money, equipment, or previous learning opportunities. Think about the newest teachers, whether they're new to the profession or new to your work setting. How does your leadership benefit these teachers and children?

What cultural values influence your expectations of a leader? How do your expectations compare with those of teachers from other cultural groups?

Other Terms Used to Discuss Leadership

One of the reasons there are so many definitions of *effective leaders* and *leadership* is that the other terms we use alongside *leadership* cause confusion. Terms that are often used to discuss leadership include *power, authority, status,* and *management*. When these terms are used in place of *leadership*, people's feelings about leadership are affected. For example, someone who equates leadership with management may think of leadership as dull and boring if that's the association they have with the term *management*. In focusing on power, authority, status, and management, we often make the mistake of locating leadership outside of the classroom or family child care setting. Let's look at what each of the four terms mean, particularly in relation to leadership.

POWER

Leadership is not merely power. *Power,* in its most casually accepted definition, can be described as an intentional, purposeful act in which one person uses some form of advantage to influence the behavior of another person. *Power* is often understood as a negative term in early care and education. This connotation may exist because we are unfamiliar with the many ways that power can be used in positive ways.

Power can be used on, for, or with another person. Power used *on* or *over* someone is simply oppression, since the follower is not provided with choices or options. Power used *for* someone is facilitation—opportunities, choices, and options are provided, and the other person makes the decision. Power used *with* someone is empowerment—you and the other person learn and succeed together—which is a very important part of leadership because each person can contribute unique gifts and abilities to accomplish a shared or common goal.

AUTHORITY

Leadership is not simply having authority. A person in authority is the one who has the right to make certain decisions. This right may come from a variety of sources, including an elected or appointed position, age (as in a family situation), or a professional position within a group or organization. A leader may possess authority, but a person in authority is not necessarily a leader. A person with authority may have the right to make a decision, but that doesn't mean she will make the right decision!

STATUS

Leadership is not the same as having status. People with status may be merely the people who occupy top positions within an organization. Status doesn't always determine leadership ability. There are people who work at the top levels of every field who couldn't lead a group of five-year-olds to ice cream. All leaders have some form of status, but not all of those who have status can be called effective leaders.

MANAGEMENT

Is leadership the same as management? An ongoing debate rages over the similarities and differences between management and leadership. For many, the two terms are interchangeable; they're seen as two different words for the same process. For others the terms describe a difference in the way an individual will perceive situations, interact with people, solve problems, and direct the group or organization. Leaders and managers can serve very different functions and purposes, but one without the other can be a setup for failure. The Leadership-Management chart shows some of the ways management and leadership differ from each other.

Management	Leadership
Provides consistency and order	Produces forward movement in an organization
Keeps an operation on time and on budget over the long haul	Creates significant change
Provides the operating talent necessary to keep an organization focused on the day-to-day tasks that must be completed for objectives to be met	Provides the conceptual talent necessary to see the historical perspective (both past and future) that facilitates growth, change, and innovation
Provides efficiency in climbing the ladder of success	Determines whether the ladder is leaning against the right wall

To the children we care for, all grown-ups have authority, status, and power. How you use yours matters. I've spent some time explaining all of these terms because you will find them used often when people talk about leadership. As you think about your own leadership development, focus on what authority, status, and power you have, what each term means to you, and how you tend to use them. The best leaders are those who tap into the human desire to have purpose in life. Increasingly, people look for purpose in the workplace, and the best leaders assist them in fulfilling their potential.

Think about a leadership situation in which you were involved or that you observed. Was the interaction based on power, authority, status, or management? How? From a leadership perspective, what might have made the outcome different?

How have you used power? Authority? Status? Management?

Describe situations in which you used power *on or over*, *for*, and *with* someone. Why did you use power in these situations? What were the outcomes? What were the other people's responses?

Functions of Leadership

The functions of leadership should tell you and those around you what you want to happen as a result of your leadership. The function is the goal of your leadership.

Three leadership functions will be discussed:

- Transformational leadership, which changes both the leader and the follower into better people and better leaders

- Situational leadership, which changes when the situation or needs change

- Servant leadership, which puts leaders in the position of serving others

Naturally, many more functions of leadership exist. The ones discussed here are primary examples and will introduce you to some of the language and literature of leadership functions. In chapter 5, you'll learn about transactional leadership, another leadership function that plays an important role in building coalitions with other organizations.

Transformational Leadership

Leadership can be transformational—changing, motivating, and elevating both leaders and followers in ways that improve society and prepare children and adults to participate in the leadership process. Transformational leaders are usually charismatic, inspirational, intellectually stimulating, and empathetic. To become a transformational leader, you must focus on influencing and inspiring others to create change as well as provide a vision and work effectively with complexity, ambiguity, and uncertainty.

Transformational leadership is constantly needed, because you can't solve complex problems once and for all. The current transformational change becomes the new static pattern, and today's solutions become tomorrow's problems. Keep this in mind as you develop your leadership ability. The change you create today will be great for solving today's problems, but tomorrow will bring new problems, and the current solution will become obsolete.

Ask Yourself

Select a typical workday and review it from beginning to end. What specific events of the day would you describe as transformational? How were these events transformational? Why?

What actions, behaviors, beliefs, and dreams do you think increase your ability to transform yourself, others, and your work environment?

Think back on a problem that existed in your work environment a couple of years ago, one that resulted in a change in how things were done. In what ways has that change created a new set of problems or stopped working now? If you could do one thing to solve the new problem, what would that be? Why might it work?

SITUATIONAL LEADERSHIP

Leadership can be situational. Sometimes circumstances and factors in a given situation determine who will emerge as a leader. Your leadership may emerge as a result of time, place, and circumstance. Rosa Parks is a familiar example. She chose an apt moment to put her years of leadership training and experience to work when she sat down in the front (whites-only section) of a bus. On that day, her leadership was needed. The time, place, and circumstance called for her to rise to the occasion. Once you experience effective leadership in one situation, you'll find it easier to recognize other leadership opportunities, and you'll be more comfortable taking on increased leadership roles.

ASK YOURSELF

Think about a situation in which an immediate decision was needed and you were the only one available to make it. How did you feel? What thoughts went through your mind? Did you make the decision? If yes, describe the steps that led to the decision. If no, explain why not. What would you do differently now? Why?

SERVANT LEADERSHIP

Leadership can mean serving others. Servant leaders in early childhood education are those who see themselves as serving coworkers, children, and their families. Servant leaders do not focus much on their own needs and goals; they focus on the needs and goals of others. If your family child care program is designed to meet your personal goals and fulfill your personal vision, it may be utilizing a form of leadership, but it is not utilizing servant leadership. If your family child care program is designed to meet the goals and visions of the families who leave their children in your care, it is utilizing servant leadership. A servant leader can be the official head of a child care setting or simply the person who keeps everyone else on a path toward the goal you all hope to achieve. Becoming a servant leader or a servant follower is not easy. It requires that each of us determine what actions and behaviors are most likely to benefit those who are being served and that the least fortunate of those served perceives himself as better off as a result of those actions and behaviors.

ASK YOURSELF

In what ways does your child care program serve coworkers, children, and their families?

How do you lead and serve children and their families?

How well served are the least privileged children and families in your work setting?

Styles of Leadership

If the function of your leadership indicates your goal, the style of your leadership should tell you and those around you the way you will carry out your leadership. Your style suggests why the situation demands a leader. Your style involves the methods you use to achieve your result.

Your leadership style is the process you use to monitor, guide, coach, direct, and evaluate the work of others. Your leadership style, much like your teaching style, will be greatly influenced by your values and beliefs about how people (children and adults) grow, develop, and change.

We'll discuss two leadership styles:

- Directive style, which involves a lot of instruction and guidance

- Facilitative style, which involves acting only in ways that improve others' performance

As is the case with leadership functions, many other styles of leadership exist as well. The two discussed here tend to show up most regularly in early childhood settings.

DIRECTIVE LEADERSHIP

A directive style may be mistaken for an authoritarian style, but they're not the same. An authoritarian style focuses primarily on the completion of the task, sometimes at the expense of the learner's needs. Someone who uses the authoritarian style gives orders, not advice, and expects those orders to be carried out without question or hesitation. In a classroom, an authoritarian teacher presents the information or content expecting that the child will learn without question or hesitation. Most of us have been in situations where someone talked or gave a lecture with no learner interaction or participation and then had the nerve to call it teaching. An authoritarian leadership style is used among adults in the military; people in the military are often expected to follow orders from a supervisor or commanding officer without question or discussion.

A directive leadership style often is used when an individual or group is performing some new task. When children are learning a new task, much direction, guidance, monitoring, and feedback are needed. You need to be involved in the task almost as much as the child. The same is true of a directive leadership style when you are interacting with adults. If a coworker is learning a new task, you will need to spend almost as much time on the task as the learner. Providing step-by-step instructions, watching as the task is performed the first few times, giving feedback on the learner's progress, and offering helpful changes are methods used in a directive leadership style.

In a classroom, the teacher provides some direction and guidance as well as opportunities for children to develop internal monitoring and responsibility. The trick is to determine whether this approach is something you use all the time, which makes it a distinct personal style, or is something you use only until the learner has mastered the task, which makes it a style you use when appropriate as a part of situational leadership.

FACILITATIVE LEADERSHIP

A facilitative leadership style provides group members with the means, resources, authority, and responsibility to act in the best interest of those affected. A facilitative style is never authoritarian, but it may be directive at times. A facilitative leader always strives to meet the needs of coworkers, children, and their families, much as servant leadership does. The facilitative style focuses on the individual strengths of each person and encourages and develops each person's leadership ability. The facilitative teacher, of course, is similarly focused, providing children with the means, resources, and authority to be active participants in the teaching and learning process while understanding her own role as a learner and the children's roles as teachers. Facilitative teachers and leaders are intentional about sharing control and aware of the importance of understanding their roles as learners. In a facilitative teaching environment, emergent curriculum occurs when the teacher uses the emerging interests, questions, and skills of the children to modify and change the original lesson plan. Facilitative leadership occurs when leaders look for and use the emerging interests, questions, and skills of others as focal points for increasing leadership.

Think about how you can vary your leadership function and style to meet the needs or experience levels of your coworkers. People who are new to a job or who are performing a new task may need more monitoring, guidance, and direction. A directive leadership style is appropriate in that situation. Those who have been performing a task for a long time may do better if left to do what they do best; a facilitative leadership style will probably work better for them. Coworkers may need extra opportunities to learn new perspectives and understand new values and priorities. They may need more time for their ideas and beliefs to form or change. When you look at leadership, remember that there is no best way to lead. Instead, you must adapt your leadership function and style to the needs of the group. This is exactly like taking a developmental approach to children's learning. Developmentally appropriate practice applies to leadership as well!

Leadership Development and Human Development

Leadership development, human development, and life experiences are interrelated processes that help make us who we are. Human development is the process by which we change cognitively, socially, intellectually, and physically as we mature. Leadership development is the process by which we increase our ability to create and influence change, growth, and achievement. Life experiences are those factors, events, and circumstances that define who we are and influence how we see the world.

Human development and leadership development involve an evolution, a transformation that changes who we are over time. This change is both qualitative and quantitative. Through your life experiences, the quality of what you know or can do becomes different—you do not simply add to the number of things you know or can do. When a child learns to dress himself, he learns over time how to put on a shirt, underwear, pants, socks, and shoes. This is quantity. He also learns over time how to dress more neatly or to coordinate his clothing. This is quality.

Becoming a leader is also a developmental process and requires that you create and interpret your own life experiences and knowledge. Some early childhood theorists call this *constructivism*. Like human development, leadership development takes time and is never finished. Leadership development is individual—it differs depending on personality, life stage, and other circumstances. Who you are as a leader integrates your previous and current selves and the new you that will continue to emerge as you learn, grow, and gain experience. You will discover and invent your own way of leading. In many ways, you have no other choice; you are a unique individual and no other person can be you better than you can.

Your beliefs and theories about how people learn, grow, and are affected developmentally will influence your beliefs and theories about leadership development. As you think about leadership development, you will have to clarify the theories you hold as a teacher and a leader. Your ability to articulate your beliefs to others will increase your thoughtfulness, your intent, your consistency, and your results.

Ask Yourself

You may be very familiar with the concepts of the teachable moment and emergent curriculum. Think about how you would recognize, take advantage of, or provide a lead-able moment. How might facilitative leadership be worked into what you do?

How will your leadership development be affected by your beliefs and theories about how children grow and learn?

ASSIMILATION AND ACCOMMODATION

Child development offers useful links to leadership development. For example, children use assimilation and accommodation when confronted with new knowledge. They assimilate new knowledge when they first learn that not every four-legged animal is a doggie. They begin to accommodate new knowledge when they develop a second category for four-legged animals: cow. Through the years, children repeatedly assimilate to accommodate the many four-legged animals in our world.

Through our own processes of assimilation and accommodation, we can transfer our current knowledge about child development to our emerging knowledge about leadership development. Multitasking, coordinating different senses, and developing competencies are just three examples of teaching skills that translate into leadership skills. As we discuss each, think about what you already do well as a teacher and how you can use those same skills as a leader.

Multitasking

Multitasking takes place when you engage in more than one activity at the same time, when you make use of more than one skill simultaneously. Some teachers think they are not good at multitasking, but in reality most people are experts at it. They have simply become so proficient at certain skills that they fail to remember they require more than one action or one skill at a time. Take learning to write a paragraph in English; children must make simultaneous use of many skills:

- Remembering the correct symbol (letter) used to make a specific sound

- Choosing correctly between similar symbols (such as b/d and p/q)

- Putting the symbols in a specific order so they represent correctly spelled words

- Focusing on the idea or story they are telling while they put several words together in sentences

Most children can do all of these things simultaneously and quickly by age eight. By the time we are adults, we can perform the multiple tasks involved in writing and reading so quickly that we come to see them as a single fluid task.

Leadership is also about multitasking. In any leadership situation, we must simultaneously

- Think about the purpose of our actions and how those actions relate to the goals and directions of the group

- Balance the needs and relationships of the people involved with the needs and requirements of the tasks to be completed

- Be able to hold onto our vision of the future while focusing on what needs to be done today

As with reading and writing, the ultimate goal in leadership development is to eventually perform these multiple tasks so quickly that leadership becomes a single fluid process.

Coordinating Different Senses

Children coordinate many different senses when they play in and explore their world. They taste the toy and make sense of it orally and manually. They see the toy and listen to the sounds it makes as it is tasted and held. They smell the toy and experience a feeling of satisfaction and happiness with the whole experience. Similarly, as adults, we coordinate many different senses when we take part in a leadership situation. We see the dynamics and the individual facial and body expressions of other people. We sense the energy of the group, the individual, or the situation. We hear the words and the tone of what is being said. Much like a child coordinating different senses, as adults we coordinate different leadership skills to accomplish things or to master new skills.

Developing Competency over Time

Being patient with your developing competency is critical to your leadership development. Children feel good about themselves and their abilities when they believe they are competent at doing what is important to them and when they believe they can compete equally with their peers. Feelings of incompetence come when children repeatedly fail at something or when they are told that they aren't capable. A very perceptive and bright child once described the difference between gifted and special education: "in the gifted classes, teachers find out what you are good at and let you do it again and again and again. In the special education classes, teachers find out what you can't do and make you do it over and over and over."

Feelings of competence and incompetence affect your leadership development. You will feel incompetent while you are practicing and learning some skills. Reflection will be key. As you repeat various skills and learn new ones, think about the result, the consequences of your words and actions.

ASK YOURSELF

Did things turn out the way you expected? Are you getting better? Can you tell?

When do you feel competent? Is it when you believe that others think you are capable of succeeding? Why do you feel that way? In what ways do the opinions of others influence your sense of competence?

When do you feel incompetent? Is it when you believe that others do not think you are capable of succeeding? Why do you feel that way? In what ways do the opinions of others influence your sense of incompetence?

Think about the natural stages of development as you build or construct your knowledge of leadership practice, and take baby steps in your leadership development journey. Through our knowledge of childhood and adolescent development, we know that there are various stages at which humans strive to construct an identity—a clear understanding of who we are, why we are, and how we want to be in the world. The same holds true in the developmental process of becoming a leader. Just as babies understand words long before they can actually talk, you will understand many leadership concepts long before you can apply them. Your first attempts may feel like baby talk ("All broke," "Me bite," or "Kitty bye-bye"). With practice and patience, your leadership attempts will become more complex ("The cup is broken," "I bit the apple," or "The cat is gone"). At some point, you will arrive at the adolescent stage of leadership. At that stage, it may be helpful to ask yourself the following questions:

- Who am I as a leader?

- What am I good at?

- What do I believe in?

- What groups do I belong to?

- What do others think of me?

- What do I believe about what they think?

The details of our individual lives are a constant part of each learning environment and each leadership environment. Education and learning are social processes that can be used to maintain or change the status quo. In the same way, leadership can be used to domesticate people to do as instructed or to liberate them to question situations and circumstances and make decisions for themselves. Who you are and who you become as a leader will be evident in how other adults and children grow and change as a result of your leadership role.

Developing Your Personal Definition of Leadership

Your thinking about leadership will become the basis for how you make decisions and what you expect of others. But in the end, how you define leaders and leadership will not be as important as how others are affected by who you are and what you do. Others will come to know your definition of a leader and leadership by the results and consequences of their interactions with you. How will they define you?

Don't be too concerned about deciding which leadership function or style is perfect for you. Just as you would use a combination of strategies to inform your work with children, you'll need a combination of strategies to inform your leadership. A perfect leader combines all the leadership functions and styles. Because leadership is complex, dynamic, interactive, and situational, no best way exists to develop or strengthen the many skills, abilities, and competencies needed. Those who can best respond in a variety of leadership situations (such as curriculum quality, political analysis, family involvement, mentoring, creative problem solving) will be those who have taken advantage of a variety of leadership-growth opportunities (such as classes, role models, volunteer experiences, books, observations, reflection). As time and experience add up, your leadership skill and ability will be transformed into a whole new leadership strength that is uniquely yours.

> What is your definition of *leader*? Of *leadership*? How did
> you arrive at these definitions?

Summary

This chapter has introduced you to some definitions, roles, and challenges of leaders and leadership. It has also discussed various leadership functions and styles and how they look in the leadership process. Through your examination of leadership development and human development, you have had many opportunities to begin reflecting on how to make links between the two and to begin transferring your skill and ability from one arena to another. In chapter 2, you will look even deeper into who you are and how you learn to be a leader. What role does family play in the development of leadership strength and ability? How do your life experiences and your culture combine to create the leader who is uniquely you? Chapter 2 will cover all of this and provide ideas for how you can stretch yourself.

STORY TIME

Tilman was the teacher in the toddler room and had just begun working with a new assistant, seventeen-year-old Lori. Those first few days with Lori had been a little frustrating for Tilman because Lori seemed to need a lot of guidance and direction, and there was really no time for that with so many active youngsters. On the third day, Tilman went home and plopped tiredly onto her couch.

"Tough day?" asked her husband.

"Yeah," Tilman replied. "I wish Lori would just do what I tell her to do instead of asking me questions about what to do all day long!"

"It must be like working with a two-year-old," her husband responded.

Tilman thought about that for the rest of the evening. The next day at work, Tilman approached Lori in a whole new way. Her husband was right: working with someone who was new to a position was like working with a two-year-old. Lori was simply in the early developmental stages of learning about her new job and her role, and early developmental stages required guidance, modeling, and direction until the behavior was internalized. Tilman needed to adjust her style to accommodate Lori's level of maturity in this new role. After two or three days of intense supervision by Tilman, Lori was off and running on her own and felt competent to do what was expected of her.

More Reading

Bass, Bernard, and Ralph M. Stogdill. 1990. *Bass and Stogdill's handbook of leadership: Theory, research, and managerial applications.* 3rd ed. New York: Free Press.

Bruno, Holly Elissa. 2009. *Leading on purpose: Emotionally intelligent early childhood administration.* Boston: McGraw-Hill Higher Education.

Etzioni, Amitai. 1991. *A responsive society: Collected essays on guiding deliberate social change.* San Francisco: Jossey-Bass.

Graham, John. 2005. *Stick your neck out: A street-smart guide to creating change in your community and beyond: Service as the path of a meaningful life.* San Francisco: Berrett-Koehler.

Greenleaf, Robert K., and Larry C. Spears. 2002. *Servant leadership: A journey into the nature of legitimate power and greatness.* 25th anniversary ed. New York: Paulist Press.

Kagan, Sharon L., and Barbara T. Bowman, eds. 1997. *Leadership in early care and education.* Washington, DC: National Association for the Education of Young Children.

Samovar, Larry A., and Richard E. Porter, eds. 2008. *Intercultural communication: A reader.* 12th ed. Belmont, CA: Wadsworth.

T'Shaka, Oba. 1990. *The art of leadership.* Richmond, CA: Pan African Publications.

Zeece, Pauline Davey. 2003. Power lines: The use and abuse of power in child care programming. In *The art of leadership: Managing early childhood organizations.* Rev. ed. Eds. Bonnie Neugebauer and Roger Neugebauer, 25–29. Redmond, WA: Child Care Information Exchange.

Chapter 2

▲

Who, Me, a Leader?

Y ou might be surprised at how early you began developing your leadership ability. Many people wonder whether leaders are born or made. Do strong leaders possess genes and family dynamics that set them up for future leadership potential? Or do potential leaders evolve as a result of life experiences combined with leadership development and training? Leaders are both born and made. They develop as a combination of both. We were all born with some natural strengths, gifts, and abilities—things we do effortlessly, without much thought. On the other hand, we all have skills and abilities that are the result of practice, hard work, and training. Most leaders find that their greatest achievements and effectiveness come when they combine natural ability and trained skill.

This chapter is designed to help you reflect on the following:

- The ways your own skills and abilities have been influenced by your family experience

- The ways you as a parent or adult family member develop and use leadership skills and abilities in your interactions with children

- The ways culture, life experiences, and learning preferences influence the type of leadership skills you develop

- The ways good leadership and good teaching require the same kinds of skills, competencies, and characteristics

Family as a Context for Leadership

Why is it important to understand how you developed and use leadership within your family? All of us take into the workplace the skills and abilities we learned growing up. Many people don't know how the leadership styles and skills they use in their interactions with family members relate to leadership on the job, but the connection is nonetheless there. If we are to strengthen and develop the best of these skills, we must first understand that we have them. Making apparent the relationship between leadership at home and leadership at work helps us strengthen those skills that are effective and recognize areas for growth.

An important point to remember about family is that all types of families can supply the components necessary for a flourishing, functioning family environment. Healthy, happy children can be found wherever there is access to the resources and services they need. *Family,* as used in this book, refers to married heterosexual parents and children, single mothers and fathers and children, single cohabiting parents and children, gay and lesbian couples, married or not, with children, adult singles or couples and their parents or other older relatives with children, singles or couples raising their grandchildren or the children of relatives, older siblings raising younger siblings, foster parents with unrelated children, and circles of friends who consider themselves a family. Any of these kinds of families can raise children effectively. Children and adults from all these kinds of families display leadership strengths and skills.

Many of the leadership characteristics and strengths that come naturally to you were already evident in your childhood. The following questions will help you think about your strengths.

ASK YOURSELF

> **As a child, were you described as achievement oriented?**
> **Did people find you sociable, reliable, or encouraging?**
>
> **What leadership skills and abilities seem to come to you naturally?**
>
> **What leadership skills and abilities have you been working on, practicing, or studying?**

> **Think about your own family experience growing up. What strengths and skills did you begin to develop as a young child? What skills were always a challenge for you?**
>
> **List three strengths or skills that seemed to come naturally to you as a child. How does each one add to your leadership skill and ability today?**

How a family is structured and what place an individual has in her family also affects how she might show leadership. Birth order and family size, economics, culture, and expectations are all factors that can affect a person's approach to leadership.

BIRTH ORDER AND FAMILY SIZE

Firstborn and last-born children tend to show more leadership ability early on. Firstborn children often benefit from early, more personal interactions with adults and adult language, and they are likely to be given more responsibility and are expected to mature faster than their younger siblings. This is particularly true with the oldest girl in low-income families or families with working mothers. My own childhood serves as an example. As the oldest of six children, I was expected to help my stay-at-home mother with the younger children. My first babysitting responsibility came at age six! When my mother needed to run to the store just two blocks away, she would put my younger siblings in front of the television. I sat behind them. Their job was to watch television. My job was to watch them.

Youngest children, on the other hand, tend to be more disobedient and persistent and are often disregarded when family or personal decisions are made. Because of this, youngest children often challenge the status quo, persist in their efforts to change things, and insist on being a part of decision-making teams later in life. As leaders, youngest children tend to take notice of how they are (or are not) involved in making decisions and when their input is blocked or ignored. They are also more persistent in having clear processes in place that keep power distributed among the members of a team. As leaders, the youngest children of larger families are more likely to try new and different things. This tendency is the result of rarely having the opportunity to be the first in the family to do something, such as take first steps, ride a bike, or learn to whistle. By the time the third or fourth child learns to whistle, the novelty has worn off for parents, so these children grow up eager to be the first to do something praiseworthy or interesting.

Middle children tend to show more variety in their leadership development, depending on the gender and age configurations of their family. In families where the middle child is the only girl and particularly if she is close in age to her older brother, she will take on more of the characteristics of the oldest girl. If she is close in age to her younger brother, she may instead take on characteristics of the youngest child, especially if the family environment tends to be more patriarchal. Many middle children, however, are just that—not the youngest and not the oldest. Middle children tend to be more adventuresome, often take more risks, and exhibit more independent behavior as a result of their need to establish an identity based on something other than being oldest or youngest. As leaders, middle children are likely to try on different roles and demonstrate leadership flexibility, using the same skills to shift roles as they did in childhood.

Only children are very similar to oldest children in their leadership development; they show more leadership ability early on, having benefitted from the early, more personal interactions with adults and adult language, having more responsibility, and being expected to mature faster. The only child also has more opportunities to develop a sense of self-sufficiency and independence. The drawback is that only children may not have the same social and emotional development experiences that children with siblings have. As leaders, only children may have to work harder at such leadership necessities as teamwork and collaboration. However, their sense of self-confidence and their self-esteem tend to be higher than those of children with siblings.

The size of your family also influenced your leadership development. Children with three or four siblings tend to work better in groups, attempting to achieve group goals. Those from smaller or larger families are more inclined to work better on an individual basis for an individual goal.

ASK YOURSELF

Are you the oldest, the only, the youngest, or the middle sibling in your family? What leadership skills did you

- **learn because of your position? What are the leadership challenges you face because of birth order?**

- **Which leadership skills do you share in common with your siblings? Which skills are unique to you? Why do you think this is so?**

- **How has family size influenced your leadership development?**

FAMILY CULTURE

The more you understand the leadership implications of culture and other differences, the easier it will become for you to make room for other perspectives in your work with children. In many ways, the more you understand and create diversity, the easier your work becomes because children, families, communities, and coworkers are likely to increase their collaborative efforts with you.

Culture influences the expectations and roles within the family and the family's relationship to the larger community. For example, the strong kinship bonds and mother-child relationships of African families are evident in the strong roles of mothers and grandmothers in African American culture. For many Asians and Asian Americans, family and community needs may take priority over the needs of individuals. In more traditional Native American families, ownership and sharing are markedly different than in European American families. In each of these communities and many others, cultural influences will determine both parental and leadership expectations and roles.

The historical experiences of cultural groups also play a role in leadership development within the family. Cultures that have been subjected to oppression or socioeconomic injustice develop family groups that are more collective and collaborative, as seen in the pooling of resources practiced by immigrant groups. These experiences can result in the pooling of leadership resources as well; leadership is more likely to be shared, and children skilled in collaboration and community building are more likely to have leadership opportunities. Caregiving tasks are also shared, especially in cultures in which families have been separated by slavery, economics, war, or death. Children living in oppression can also learn important leadership skills from having endured these circumstances, such as courage, dependability, empathy, and integrity. Parents begin teaching children how to recognize these traits and characteristics early on as basic survival skills. Understanding the cultural differences will increase your ability to understand the context in which leadership in families develops. Families in different circumstances will foster and focus on different leadership skills. When families from different cultural and historical experiences come together in the workplace, they bring a diverse set of skills to leadership.

Culture also influences the ways adults and children interact with each other. A good parent may be expected to tend to a crying baby immediately or to wait to see if the fussiness passes. A good parent may be expected to engage in much physical play with a child or in quiet, less physical activities. A good parent may be expected to do all of the above, depending on the situation. As you continue to think about what it means to be a good teacher and leader of young children, keep in mind that there are many ways to be a good leader and many ways to interact with children and adults. Paying attention to what makes a good leader in different cultures will help you increase your own leadership skill and ability.

Challenges and differing opinions arise about children's socialization when children are not members of the dominant cultural group. Some feel that children should be taught the values, skills, abilities, and behaviors that will help them fit in better with the dominant culture. Others believe it is better to ensure that children maintain the traditional cultural patterns that help them become model citizens within their cultural group and community. Still others are more inclined toward biculturalism for their children—helping them become empowered members of both cultural groups. Our role as developing leaders is to understand a variety of cultural patterns and their impact on our leadership skills, abilities, and strengths.

The families and communities served by your early childhood program have their own family leadership experiences and expectations; they may expect a certain kind of leadership from you. Part of your leadership development should focus on increasing your understanding of the many ways families' cultural expectations influence their leadership expectations.

What have you learned about leadership in the family through your culture? What have you learned through your group's or community's historical experience?

Adults of different cultures also vary in the ways they communicate and interact with adults, peers, and others. What communication and interaction skills have you learned from your culture? What skills are you lacking?

In your own family, what cultural leadership skills have you learned? What skills are you passing on to the next generation?

How do your teaching practices reflect the children's home communities and the communities' expectations for their children?

Family Expectations

Families play an essential role as the birthplace for potential leadership; so many of our current leadership characteristics, skills, and abilities had their beginnings in our families. Confidence, self-esteem, and assertiveness, for example, are often developed with family and are important characteristics in recognizing leadership opportunities and being able to take advantage of them. Each of these characteristics may develop early in children but may be specific to certain situations. As a child, you may have been confident in one area but not in another or confident with one group of people but not with another. If you grew up in a family that spoke a language other than English, you may have been more confident and assertive when expressing your feelings at home than at school. As a child, you were developing the leadership skills you would use as an adult, but you may have used those skills more often with one group (family) than with another (school).

The family can set the expectations for its children's achievements and success in both positive and negative ways, making it possible for children from very different family environments to develop the same leadership traits. For example, the motivation to lead and succeed may result from a home with a very loving atmosphere, praising that stresses risk taking, a home with consistently high expectation and very little love, or a home in which a child was told she wouldn't amount to much so she had to succeed just to prove her family wrong. Look for and cultivate the leadership potential in each and every family experience regardless of family circumstances. You never know where a future leader may emerge.

The absence or presence of confidence, self-esteem, and assertiveness also influences the roles children play or avoid and the leadership they assert as adults. Leadership characteristics, skills, and ability begin in the family but develop when children are exposed to divergent or conflicting viewpoints and experiences outside the family in child care centers, schools, community and religious organizations, and community culture.

ASK YOURSELF

Where did you find confidence as a child? Where was your confidence lacking? Below are some suggestions to get you started. Add more of your own.

- **Making art**
- **Doing math**
- **Caring for pets**
- **Drama/pretend playing**
- **Doing schoolwork**
- **Storytelling**
- **Inventing things**
- **Science experimenting**
- **Swimming**
- **Biking**
- **Jumping rope**
- **Learning languages**
- **Creating games**

- **Giving advice**
- **Caring for others**
- **Playing basketball**

People want to hear what potential leaders have to say and what they think. When you were young, in what situations did other children or adults listen to you or seek out your opinions and advice?

Parenting and Leading

Strong connections can be made between what leaders do and what adults who have or work with children do. What is parenting? Simply put, parenting is the way we prepare children to meet the expectations and challenges of their communities and to understand their society and culture. If you do not have children, you still influence children's development as community members through teaching and example.

The concept of parent leadership assumes that all parents are leaders for their children and use a complex set of leadership knowledge and skills. Not every parent is born with leadership ability, and most do not gain it immediately when they become responsible for a child. The role of the parent as a family leader is dynamic, a process of human development for both adults and children. Parents and children grow and change together, supporting and challenging each other as they play out their lives together.

ASK YOURSELF

Potential leaders think about their natural gifts and talents, the things they do best. What do you do best? What natural gifts and talents do you possess? How do you use these talents? If you don't use them, why don't you?

Ask your children what they think are your leadership strengths and weaknesses. Ask them what they think theirs are.

In the big picture of parenting, many leadership functions are performed:

- Finding and organizing resources

- Cultivating children's intellects, interests, and talents

- Setting expectations for children's successes

- Influencing children's self-esteem through demonstrations of love and praise

- Providing basic necessities, such as food and shelter

- Ensuring adequate health care, quality child care, a good education, and a safe environment

In many ways, parents serve as the first "case managers" for their children. They are responsible for finding, organizing, and managing all the resources their children need for healthy development in every domain: physical, social, cognitive, and emotional.

On a daily basis, parents use a variety of leadership skills and strategies with their children and other family members. Consider the following list of leadership tasks, and give one example of how you have used each:

- **Planning** activities and events for family gatherings or outings

- Creating **team-building** activities to strengthen family bonds

- **Negotiating** with children and other family members to reach agreements

- **Scheduling** the day to accommodate children's school and recreational activities

- **Modeling** appropriate behavior based on family values and preferences

- **Arbitrating** disagreements between siblings

- **Setting goals** to afford a family vacation

- **Supervising** children in their work, play, and interactions with others

- **Setting performance expectations** for children's chores and behavior

- **Motivating** children and other family members to accomplish tasks

- **Understanding group dynamics** to effectively influence how family members respond to each other

- Using **problem-solving** strategies to help children figure out what went wrong with a project

- **Making decisions** based on current information or past results

- **Strategizing** ways to get through tough times

- Using **multitasking** skills to cook dinner, supervise homework, and finish one more load of laundry simultaneously

By substituting *leader* for *parent, staff* for *family,* and *employees* for *children* or *siblings,* you can begin to see the parallels between leadership in the workplace and the family. Parents use leadership styles in their families in the same way leaders do in other groups. Compare, for example, the parent who views a child's questions as a sign of disrespect to the supervisor who reprimands an employee for asking too many questions. Compare, as another example, the parent who involves the child in solving a family problem to the supervisor who involves employees in solving a work problem.

FAMILY LEADERSHIP STYLES

Let's take a look at three families camping together. The first set of parents uses what seems to be a hands-off style of leadership: family members do whatever they feel like doing; and the children run free with no structures, rules, or guidelines. The second set of parents uses a participative style of leadership: all family members have a part in each activity, and each activity is planned and carried out collectively with guidelines and set boundaries. The third set of parents uses an authoritarian style: the parents determine activities and assign tasks without a lot of input from the children and expect tasks to be completed effectively and efficiently.

The three styles are very different and reflect the different ideas each family has about what makes a camping experience fun. The first set of parents thinks camping is fun because all rules are put aside. The second set thinks camping is fun because parents and children spend time together and learn to work as a team. The third set thinks camping is fun because everything is organized and efficient. The leadership provided by each set of parents is designed to meet the goals and values they have established for their families. As you can see, even though the goal of having fun is the same for each family, the style of leadership used to achieve the goal can be very diverse.

Different parenting styles are influenced by culture and community as well. Hands-off parenting may be used to encourage children to discover their environment for themselves, or it may reflect a desire to raise self-reliant children. It also may be used only in certain situations, such as camping. Parenting that is shared with children may reflect egalitarian values in which all have a say, or it may reflect the desire of an individual to raise fully empowered children. Firm, directive parenting may be the result of surviving in an oppressive society, or it may reflect a desire to maintain traditional values of respect and obedience. The important point to remember is that different parenting styles reflect different leadership styles and involve different leadership skills, which parents implement in rearing and socializing their young.

Ask Yourself

What was the leadership style in your family when you were growing up? What impact did it have on your own leadership development? What leadership style do you use in your current family? What impact does it have on each family member?

How did your family's theory of child development affect your leadership development? How did your family's beliefs about how children should be raised affect your leadership development?

Think about the family of a childhood friend. In what ways were your two families different? In what ways were they alike? What leadership skills and abilities do you think were developing in your friend's family?

Think for a moment about how each of these leadership styles—hands-off, participative, and authoritarian—might look in the early childhood education workplace. What would be the positive aspects of each style? What would be the negative aspects of each style?

The parent who provides meaningful assistance and guidance to a child so the child will do well in school and be admitted to college performs tasks similar to the lead teacher who assists an aide in developing new skills to become a classroom teacher. The parent who successfully manages the family budget performs tasks similar to the family child care provider who is responsible for ensuring that her business's budget stays on track. It is clear that the many duties and tasks performed by parents parallel those performed by leaders in other areas. Parents have the opportunity to grow leaders in much the same way that organizations grow leaders.

Good Teachers Make Good Leaders

Faced with a situation that demands leadership, a good teacher will often display the characteristics and skills of a good leader. Like any other leader, the teacher understands that change is inevitable and that there will always be challenges. Both teacher and leader see the opportunities and benefits in taking risks and learning from past mistakes. Both constantly reflect on their actions and beliefs and think about results and consequences. Both teacher and leader understand the importance of teaching, learning, and achieving as part of a community. These basic dispositions help create an environment in which learning and leading happen naturally. As you develop as a leader, pay attention to the characteristics, skills, and behaviors you use as a teacher, and think about how these affect your effectiveness. The following chart compares teaching competencies and the competencies that all early childhood education leaders must possess to lead and manage effective and efficient teams. Describe how you achieve the competencies in each column. Then, have someone else describe how you achieve the competencies in each column. You may be surprised by the results.

Effective ECE TEACHER Competencies	Effective ECE LEADER Competencies
Creation and Development of Organizational Culture	
Understands the curriculum and can explain it to many people in many different ways; recognizes the small steps; is involved, honest, and sincere in motives; is assertive and energetic; shows commitment or passion	Articulates organizational mission, goals, and direction; plans small wins; is a capable tribal storyteller (transmits the organization's culture); envisions the future
Written and Verbal Communication Skills	
Is people oriented, a good listener, and a good public speaker; shows consideration of others, commitment or passion, sociability, and a sense of humor	Builds networks; knows about cultural differences; builds teams; supports others; manages conflict
Analytic Problem-Solving Skills	
Balances action, theory, and reflection through a combination of work, study, and thought; is open to new perspectives; explains a problem from more than one perspective; takes risks; shows courage	Monitors, informs and clarifies; seeks opportunities
Interpersonal Skills	
Is people oriented, honest, and sincere; shows consideration of others, sociability, and a sense of humor; understands followers	Motivates and inspires others; fosters collaboration; resolves conflict; recognizes and rewards others for their achievements

Attitude and Disposition	
Shows consistency and endurance; is enthusiastic, yet humble; shows self-confidence or self-esteem; can accommodate divergent viewpoints; takes risks and shows courage	Shows flexibility, openness to change, and openness to contrary opinions; can accommodate divergent viewpoints; experiments; takes risks
Child and Family Development Knowledge	
Recognizes differences and similarities; recognizes talent in others; shows self-confidence or self-esteem; shows consideration of others; can accommodate divergent viewpoints	Knows about multiple intelligences and learning styles; is aware of different cultural perspectives on developmental values and priorities
Fiscal Management and Planning	
Shows foresight and good judgment; is honest and sincere in motives; shows consistency and endurance; is energetic or active; takes risks and shows courage	Knows about budgets; can find and allocate resources
Staff Development and Supervision	
Recognizes differences and similarities; recognizes talent in others; is enthusiastic, yet humble; shows consideration of others; can accommodate divergent viewpoints; understands followers	Solves problems; consults; is capable of telling why rather than how; delegates, plans, and organizes

Some people naturally come by the skills in this chart, while others have to consciously develop and use them. It does not matter whether you come by a leadership or teaching ability naturally or have to work at it. What matters is that you engage in each one. As with any new skill, leadership must be attempted and practiced if it is to be developed.

: **Refer to the chart on the previous two pages. In what ways**
: **do you practice the competencies in the eight categories**
: **naturally? Where do you need to improve? In what ways?**
: **What is your improvement plan?**

You may not be able to imagine yourself as the ideal early childhood education leader who uses all of the competencies and skills described in the columns of the chart. Instead, think about how many of them you do use and what you need to work on next. Certain characteristics, experiences, values, attributes, and competencies directly influence whether you will emerge as a leader within a group. The more skills, abilities, and perspectives you have, the more opportunities you will have to emerge as a leader. Persist, be patient with your leadership development, and find opportunities to practice as many of the competencies as you can. To develop, practice, and strengthen these skills, place yourself in the position of gaining a new leadership ability whenever the opportunity arises.

How Adults Learn

The process by which you acquire a leadership skill and ability is just as important as the leadership skill or ability itself. How you learn matters just as much as what you are learning. There are lots of ways to learn leadership: storytelling, rhymes, reading, practice, movement, songs, classes, books, listening to the story of a colleague, observing someone else, workshops, trial and error, reflection, dialogue, and many more. Just as a new concept must be presented to children in a number of ways if it is to be remembered and learned, new leadership skills must be preserved and practiced in a number of ways to make our leadership ability more complex, flexible, and likely to stick. Creative play is vital to children's cognitive development and is an important part of leadership as well. Play in leadership means being creative, flexible, and curious; thinking of possibilities; and taking chances. It means taking on new roles, just as children do in pretend play. Creativity can include thinking of a seemingly off-the-wall but effective solution to a problem. Flexibility can include considering someone else's idea. Thinking of possibilities can include considering the impossible. Taking chances can include letting a novice take on an important leadership function.

As early childhood professionals, we know that children learn best when they are following their own interests, making their own choices, having their own hands-on experience, and interacting with others. Adults learn best under the same circumstances, and this type of learning environment is also best for leadership development. Real growth and learning take place in the midst of confusion, excitement, disequilibrium, reflection, and practice. As children learn, they experience assimilation, which hooks new knowledge to previous knowledge, and accommodation, which reconstructs previous knowledge as new knowledge. The same will happen to you as you develop your leadership. Your previous ability will provide the links that make sense of your new skill and ability. As you become more practiced and proficient, your previous leadership ability and skill will change into something completely new and different.

Leadership opportunities should have elements of familiarity and novelty. The familiarity of the situation provides a level of comfort and competence. The process of assimilation makes it possible to link the new situation to previous learning, to something you already know and are able to do. The novelty of the situation provides the growing potential, the opportunity to make choices and decisions. The process of accommodating the novelty allows for the construction of new knowledge and the reconstruction of previous knowledge; you adjust your previous knowledge to understand something new and different. Everyone possesses knowledge and facts that are not as accurate as you might think. Just as children have to learn and unlearn a lot as they add to their knowledge and experience base, adults have to learn and unlearn a lot about leadership and what it means to lead.

As you learn, you create categories—little boxes—to put the learning in. Each experience, event, idea, action, and fact is placed in a category with other similar items. Learning needs to be both relevant and connected for learners of all ages. If what you are learning doesn't seem to have any relevance to or connection with anything in your life or your previous knowledge, the learning will not stick—it simply will not seem important to you, and you will not remember it. Later, when something happens to you that makes that learning relevant to your life, you'll have that familiar experience: "I remember someone told me something about that once, but I can't remember what it was." Now the learning becomes relevant and connected. Now you will learn and remember it. Leadership is the same way: you will learn and remember best those leadership concepts that are relevant to and connected with your previous experiences and knowledge.

ASK YOURSELF

- **How do you prefer to learn about leadership? Why?**

- **What role does play have in your leadership development?**

- **What do others say about leadership? Read books, newspapers, journals, or other written works to find out. How much of what you read applies to your own leadership interests? Don't forget to read fiction, which provides a wealth of opportunities to apply your leadership knowledge to the characters you meet there. Create opportunities to write about, reflect on, and share what you have read. Such discussions will spark further ideas and insights into what you have read, leading to deeper levels of understanding.**

- **Think of a time when you learned something new or changed your mind about something you always thought to be true. What previous learning did you assimilate? What accommodation to your previous learning did you make to reconstruct new learning?**

- **How do you recognize when a child or another adult is assimilating or accommodating new information?**

Life Experiences

Your life experiences are an integral part of your leadership development. Characteristics like age, race, physical ability, culture, socioeconomic level, educational preparedness, national origin, work experience, and career aspirations affect your life experiences. In turn, your life experiences will affect your leadership development because leadership skill, ability, and potential look different in different cultures or subgroups. Try to understand and appreciate people who have a different perspective than you, and try to understand and appreciate your own role and sense of belonging in a multicultural society.

Having lived many years, each of us brings a complex personal history to leadership. This history includes childhood, cultural, and developmental experiences; knowledge; skills; learning styles; and values, beliefs, and perceptions about ourselves and those with whom we interact. Many people have not really thought about or examined the impact or power of these factors in their lives and on their leadership. Some people have a strong sense of who they are and what they can do because they have reflected on these factors. Make sure you are one of them. Be sure to set aside time to reflect on who you are, what you think, and why.

Your development as a teacher and a leader will be affected by how much you have examined and integrated your experiences, values, and beliefs about racism, sexism, classism, homophobia, morality, the distribution of resources, and a host of other social, cultural, and political factors that make up the fabric of your world.

For example, people who value distinct and separate roles and responsibilities for men and women may view the process of and purpose for leadership very differently from those who prefer to blur the lines between gender roles. People who are used to seeing only European Americans in leadership positions may not be familiar with the way leadership looks and sounds when it comes from another culture. People who believe that most leaders have or should have access to lots of money may think that effective leadership is not readily available in poorer communities. When you have examined your beliefs, values, and experiences, you will be able to think more intentionally about what leadership means to you.

ASK YOURSELF

Who are you? How do you describe yourself?

Make a list of the key life experiences that have made the biggest impacts on how you describe yourself. Why is each

experience so meaningful to you? How has each experience influenced your view of yourself as a leader?

The same systems that affect your human development will affect your leadership development. These systems include family, school, culture, community, social-service agencies, state and federal government agencies, popular media, and social trends. How have these different systems affected your leadership development?

MOTIVATION

Leaders must be able to motivate others. Study what motivates you and what motivates those affected by your leadership. Motivation is the incentive to do, change, or accomplish something. There are two kinds of motivation: intrinsic motivation (because you want to) and extrinsic motivation (because someone or something makes you). Intrinsic motivation is more powerful and more lasting than extrinsic, because it is linked to your own interests, passions, needs, and desires. Connecting these intrinsic motivators to those of others will produce meaningful results and awesome accomplishments. Refocus on the deep longings you have for community, dignity, meaning, and love in your professional life. In general, people are motivated by creative groups and organizations—those that focus on *what* is right as opposed to *who* is right.

When you are motivated by something outside of yourself, such as money, reward, praise, and punishment, motivation is fleeting because, as everyone knows, once the extrinsic factor is removed, little incentive to continue is left. Sometimes, of course, it is necessary to apply this kind of outside motivation for a period of time until inside motivation takes over. At some point, everyone expects a child who is made to share a toy through the reward of a treat or threat of a time-out will develop the inside motivation to share because it is a caring thing to do. In developing your leadership skill and ability, you need a clear understanding of when you are motivated internally and when you are motivated by something extrinsic, such as a reward or fear of punishment.

Ask Yourself

What excites you? What makes you angry? What compels you to devote time, energy, and other resources to achieve a goal? Focusing on your interests and passions through questions like these can assist you in finding your leadership niche.

What are the interests and passions of your coworkers? What energizes them? Are they aware of their own interests and passions? How can you assist them in the same way you would like to be assisted by others?

SELF-REFLECTION

Reflection seems like such a simple matter that we sometimes forget how critical it is to leading, teaching, learning, and effecting social change. In its simplest form, reflection means looking at oneself and what one is doing—like looking in the mirror. The power of reflection comes when you do more than just glance at what you see. As a leader, you reflect on your experience to increase leadership skill and ability rather than dwell on the experience itself.

The answers to your reflections on the whys and why nots of what you do will take you to the meaningful side of reflection—the place of deep examination and critical analysis. This is an important step in personal and social change that involves theory, reflection, and action. As you read this book, you are affirming, assimilating, and accommodating knowledge. You may come across a piece of knowledge very different from what you currently believe to be true or currently understand, and you will find ways to assimilate and/or accommodate it. Later, after you've given some thought to what you have read, you may change your previous beliefs as you develop new understandings. A few days later, you may decide to try out a few of these new concepts when a leadership opportunity is presented.

How do you make time for reflection? How do you structure your reflection time? In what ways do you provide opportunities for others, such as colleagues, children, and families, to reflect?

The process of knowing yourself involves remembering, thinking about, and reflecting on past experiences. For each of us, this process includes both good and bad memories. Unless you are working with a trained professional, such as a therapist, do not spend a lot of time trying to reflect on memories that are very painful and that block your learning. Reflection as a way of developing your leadership ability should be a growing process, not one that inhibits your growth or keeps you from moving forward. This does not mean that you should avoid unhappy or unpleasant memories. Instead, simply ask yourself whether the specific memory helps your learning or blocks your learning.

EXERCISE

Here is an exercise for using reflection to reconnect with your childhood leadership ability: Select an occasion in your childhood when you served in a leadership role. It can be any occasion at any time in your childhood. Did you rally the children in your neighborhood to play a new game or hear you tell a story? Were you the captain of the school pep team? Did others seek your guidance or follow your advice? Were you the oldest of several children? Did you organize a neighborhood cleanup or food drive? Did others tend to copy your style of dress? Did you write a poem or story or create a piece of art that inspired special feelings in others?

What do you remember about this occasion? Who was there? What was the atmosphere? How did others respond? What was your favorite aspect of the experience? What was your least favorite aspect?

What messages did others give you about the experience? What did you think about these messages? What influence does this experience have on your leadership strength or ability today? Did you consider yourself a leader then? Why or why not?

Reflection on your practice of leadership can take place in ways besides asking yourself questions. Discussion with colleagues is a marvelous way to reflect. Mentoring, being mentored, observing, and being observed are also ways to increase your self-evaluation and leadership strengths. As you practice, experience more challenges, and encounter more opportunities, reflect on these. Your confidence in yourself and your ability to lead will increase.

Ask Yourself

Go back and reflect on yesterday, step by step. What did you do that worked? What did you do that didn't? How do you know? Was the outcome of your day what you intended or expected? What would you do differently the next time? Are you looking for the correct outcome, or are there other possibilities?

Do as children do! Ask "Why?" a thousand times. Pick something that you did today, and ask yourself why you did it. Whatever your answer happens to be, ask yourself why, again . . . and again . . . and again.

Summary

Getting to know who you are as a leader will require some intentional thought and dedicated time. A number of questions posed to you throughout this book encourage exploration of who you are and how you came to be you. Write each question on an individual slip of paper, and place the paper slips in a jar. If you reflect on one each day or each week, you will be amazed at how much you will learn about yourself by the time the jar is empty.

How do you learn to be a leader? You have already started by learning more about yourself and how you began developing leadership skills in your family, parenting, and teaching children. You have reflected on the influences of individual experiences, such as birth order, culture, and learning styles. In chapter 3, you will have an opportunity to learn more about the skills and qualities that make leaders effective. Where do values and vision come from? What role do you play when you make leadership decisions? How can you increase your cross-cultural competence? How will effective communication and interpersonal skills enhance your leadership? The answers are coming up soon!

STORY TIME

Cynthia decided to open a family child care program. After completing her associate's degree in early childhood education, Cynthia married Joe and delayed her potential career to raise their four children. Being a homemaker was a rewarding experience for Cynthia, but at times she thought wistfully of what life might have been like for her if she had accepted the teaching-assistant position she had been offered just after she married.

One of those times was when her oldest son, Miguel, was seven and joined the Little League team in town. Cynthia agreed to organize the carpool schedule for eight families. Then there was the time when Dolores was sixteen and decided that her father had old-fashioned views about dating. Cynthia found herself caught in the middle, torn between the need to remain the parent and the need to let her daughter grow up. She managed to help Dolores and Joe come to an agreement, but it took a while.

Cynthia was quite pleased at the way the children had grown up to become admirable adults. She and Joe had strong values about education and a commitment to the community, and although helping the children stay on top of things at school had been a challenge, Dolores was now a doctor in a neighborhood clinic, Miguel was a supervisor at the plant, Tina was a kindergarten teacher, and Joey was in the last year of his engineering program at the university. Cynthia had more time on her hands than she had experienced in a long time. Joe wouldn't retire for another five years, and the extra money Cynthia could earn by opening a family child care program would come in handy.

Cynthia decided to take a leadership class at the community center and was pleased with the book she had to read: it was all about developing and transferring leadership skills and abilities from one area of life to another area. Already, Cynthia was finding out about how she had developed leadership skills through the process of parenting. It was becoming easier and easier for her to describe to Joe her vision of a family child care program and what steps she would have to take to get there.

More Reading

Bruno, Holly Elissa. 2009. *Leading on purpose: Emotionally intelligent early childhood administration.* Boston: McGraw-Hill Higher Education.

Darder, Antonia. 1991. *Culture and power in the classroom: A critical foundation for bicultural education.* New York: Bergin and Garvey.

Isaacson, Cliff, and Meg Schneider. 2004. *The birth order effect for couples: How birth order affects your relationships and what you can do about it.* Gloucester, MA: Fair Winds Press.

Kouzes, James M., and Barry Posner. 1987. *The leadership challenge: How to get extraordinary things done in organizations.* San Francisco: Jossey-Bass.

McCaleb, Sudia Paloma. 1997. *Building communities of learners: A collaboration among teachers, students, families, and communities.* Mahwah, NJ: Lawrence Erlbaum Associates.

Nobles, Wade W., Lawford L. Goddard, and William E. Cavil. 1987. *African American families: Issues, insights, and directions.* Oakland: Institute for the Advanced Study of Black Family Life and Culture.

Spock, Benjamin, and Robert Needleman. 2004. *Dr. Spock's baby and child care.* 8th ed. New York: Pocket Books.

Stonehouse, Anne. 1995. *How does it feel? Child care from a parent's perspective.* Redmond, WA: Child Care Information Exchange.

Trawick-Smith, Jeffrey. 1997. *Early childhood development: A multicultural perspective.* Upper Saddle River, NJ: Prentice Hall.

Wynn, Mychal. 2005. *Empowering African-American males: A guide to increasing Black male achievement.* Ed. Glenn Bascome. Marietta, GA: Rising Sun.

Young, James C. 2006. *From roots to wings: Successful parenting African American style.* Chicago: African American Images.

Chapter 3

▲

The Cultural Context
of Leadership

Culture influences leadership. Communication styles, processes for interacting with others and working with conflict, and competition/cooperation and learning/knowing preferences are just a few of the areas strongly influenced by culture. Many of the characteristics listed are essential parts of leadership as well.

All people need to be able to lead and serve effectively in multicultural environments. The field of early childhood care and education is extremely diverse in terms of the people who work in the field and the families served. We must each learn how to lead a diverse group of people and learn how to be led by those who differ from us. Your leadership education and development must focus on how your cultural differences affect your perceptions of reality, what it means to serve a diverse group, how leadership is manifested in different cultures, and how you recognize, encourage, and develop your own leadership ability.

Becoming an effective leader means understanding how the world makes sense to others as well as understanding how the world makes sense to you. Your ability to do this as a teacher makes your work with children and their families more effective. You know that trying to get a three-year-old to understand that two different-sized containers can hold the same amount of water is futile. To the child, the tall glass holds more water than the shallow dish. The ability to understand the child's perspective as well as our own gives us the opportunity to create bridges for the child between his world and ours. Leadership is similar. Your ability to understand another's perspective allows you to offer solutions that make sense to others as well as you. If you suggest solutions that only make sense to you, you will be telling others that their perspectives are wrong. Leadership is about solutions that take other people's perspectives into account.

Leadership in a diverse early childhood education work environment involves leaders and followers working toward a goal, learning from each other, and drawing on the strengths they hold collectively as a result of their life experiences. The challenge for new leaders is to unlearn old mind-sets and concentrate on the potential and creativity diversity brings. In some centers and school-age programs, diversity is not a future possibility but a current reality. In other programs, more diversity exists than you may think if characteristics like age, physical ability, sexual orientation, family structure, educational experience, and socioeconomic level are taken into consideration. The combination of these differences creates a dynamic mix of leadership that can be very powerful.

In my previous position as dean of Pacific Oaks College Northwest in Seattle, I had the wonderful opportunity to experience the most multicultural, multilingual, and multiracial work environment I have ever encountered. The eighteen of us were equally balanced among four cultural groups: African American, Asian American, Latina, and European American. Languages spoken included English (American, Canadian, and Australian), four regional variations of Spanish (Mexican, Chilean, Guatemalan, and Puerto Rican), Mandarin and Cantonese, and Tigrinya (a language of Eritrea in East Africa). As you can see, even within the four cultural groups, we had a lot of cultural diversity. We were able to take the leadership strengths and expectations from all these diverse cultures to create a new kind of leadership that met most of our individual cultural needs and expectations. This gave us an incredible advantage in working with a variety of families, communities, and racial and cultural groups in Seattle. We also learned a great many new leadership skills from each other, such as how to switch leadership approaches based on the specific community we were working with and how to create teams of different racial combinations to address the needs of early childhood organizations that served more than one racial or cultural group. If your work setting currently serves diverse populations, you can increase your leadership ability and effectiveness by forming a multiracial or multicultural work team.

ASK YOURSELF

- **Think of all the ways you are different from your cowork-ers. What are the strengths and skills you bring to a lead-ership situation as a result of those differences?**

- **In what ways are your coworkers different from you? What are the strengths and skills they bring to a leadership situation?**

What Is Diversity?

Cultural diversity, pluralism, and multiculturalism include all the qualities that make people individuals. They include, but are not limited to, culture, race, color, ethnicity, gender, age, national origin, physical ability, religion, socioeconomic level, language, sexual orientation, politics, organizational philosophy, intelligence, occupational skills, and attitudes.

Diversity and difference are important concepts in leadership. No two leadership situations will be exactly the same, no one solution will address every leadership need, and no two people (or three or four) will read the same leadership situation the same way. Each person may come up with very different yet equally effective ways to proceed. Your leadership task is to notice, appreciate, and take advantage of the diversity and difference each adult brings to the leadership process. Children notice differences among people. It's their job to sort and classify—to notice racial, ethnic, gender, religious, and physical differences in other people. You can add to your leadership ability by beginning to notice differences the way children do. The more you can take advantage of cultural differences in leadership, the better chance you'll have of providing leadership that meets the needs of a diverse group of coworkers or a diverse group of children and families.

Because of your knowledge of child development, you understand that many patterns of physical development and activity exist. Not all children do exactly the same thing in exactly the same way at exactly the same time. The same is true of leadership. Your work with teachers from other cultures provides lots of opportunities to pay attention to how different people respond to leadership opportunities.

There are usually very good reasons for the unique behaviors, communication styles, expectations, and values of a culture or community. Cultural differences are not developmental deficits, and it is critical for early childhood professionals to understand this and see how the distinction affects their leadership strengths and abilities. A child who is quiet and observant is not less engaged than his outgoing, talkative counterpart. A leader who is low key and deliberate is not less effective at achieving goals than her charismatic, quick-footed counterpart.

Cultures and communities have strong convictions about what is important for their members to know, value, believe, and do. For example, we all learn to communicate with other people. Culture and community influence whether the communication is mostly verbal, with very little body movement or eye contact, all body movement (as in American Sign Language), or some combination of the two. Culture and community dictate which movements, styles, tones, and expressions are acceptable and which ones are not. Culture and community teach us which of these will feel comfortable and which ones will cause us to feel uncomfortable. In your interactions with others—coteachers and the families you serve—you will encounter a variety of communication styles. To be an effective leader and to serve different families effectively, you will need to increase your comfort with and tolerance for many ways of communicating and interacting. The work you do with children every day and the regular interactions you have with their families offer you many opportunities to practice these skills.

How you lead and how you respond to leadership situations will play a big part in your leadership development. Culture and community determine how we evaluate or define certain behaviors and how much patience and tolerance we have for certain kinds of environments. For example, what some cultures or communities define as verve or vibrancy may be interpreted by other cultures or communities as hyperactivity or overstimulation. The culture or community in which you grew up will influence your levels of patience with and tolerance for different activities or behaviors. If you grew up in a culture or community in which children and adults were relatively still, you might have less patience with the activity and volume levels of a more demonstrative culture. Your work with other teachers, children, and their families will be more effective and satisfying once you increase your comfort level with a variety of communication and interaction patterns.

For example, think of a situation when another person disagreed with you or had a different goal or result in mind. Your initial reaction to the situation was probably based on what you were taught within your culture or community. Did you continue to explain your position? Did you walk away? Did you listen carefully to what the other person was saying? Did you defend your position? Did you give in? What did you learn about the other person? What did that person learn about you?

The amount of competition and cooperation valued in your culture also influences your leadership style. This is evident even in something as simple as the types of games you played as a child. Some cultures value a high degree of competition. In these cultures, childhood games may focus on individual achievement. Rugged individualism and determining the winner are important values here. Other cultures value a high degree of collaboration and cooperation. Childhood games in these cultures may be less competitive and more collective. In these cases, all-for-one-and-one-for-all is an important value. You can increase your leadership and teaching abilities by helping your early childhood setting become an environment in which competition and cooperation can exist as equal values. Providing space for different perspectives and ways of being in the world will give each of your coworkers and children the opportunity to show what they're good at and to learn another skill at the same time.

Understanding the cultural contexts of leadership means learning how different styles of learning and knowing are emphasized or valued in different cultures. You can begin to transfer that knowledge to your understanding of how people may prefer to learn in a leadership situation. For example, African and African American cultures often place a high value on social understanding and the ability to read and write through body language, facial expressions, style, mannerisms, and tone. In a leadership environment that emphasizes this type of intelligence, you will find heightened discussion, dialogue, oratory, and dramatic expression. A leadership environment that emphasizes movement includes more physical activity, such as dance, sport, drama, and use of movement. A leadership environment in early childhood education should provide opportunities for adults and children to learn in the ways they like most. You can enact small changes that make big differences to others—changes such as adding opportunities for small-group discussions at meetings or having everyone take a walk around the block during a meeting break. Additions such as these indicate to others that you understand that they will learn better—and you will lead better—when a variety of needs are met.

Diversity will always be a part of our lives and experiences. The more you learn about diversity, the more you will understand its benefits. Should you find yourself in a situation in which little or no diversity seems visible, begin asking others what they think about various ideas or directions. Offer a different perspective, and see where it leads. Don't allow yourself or your group to fall into the trap of thinking that everyone feels the same way about something or that everyone would make the same choices or decisions. A good leader creates time and opportunities for new and different perspectives, for new and different solutions in leadership situations.

ASK YOURSELF

How does your understanding of diversity affect the work you do with children?

How has your leadership development been influenced by biology, race, psychology, gender, culture, physiology, and all the other exciting, interesting things that happen to us along the road of life?

What differences do you notice in the communication styles of your coworkers? In their expectations? In the amount of time they spend reaching a decision?

Are you the outgoing, talkative, quick-footed type of leader or the observant, low-key, deliberate type of leader? Name three advantages of your preferred leadership style. Now name three advantages of the style you did not select.

Values and Vision

Learning about leadership requires you to think about values and vision. *Values* are those beliefs, principles, and ideals that influence leaders and followers. *Vision* is perceiving and conceiving of a better place, situation, or circumstance in the future. Your vision is what you see as a better future for children, for your place of work, or even for the early childhood education profession as a whole. Your values are the guidelines that determine how you will achieve that vision—what steps or actions you will take. Values and vision are the twin pillars of effective leadership, and both are affected by culture. In a leadership situation, values and vision become a combination of who you are and what you do.

VALUES

All human beings have values. Values are the principles and beliefs you hold about what is important and how things are done. They shape how you treat people, the choices you make, and how you see life in general. Your personal values develop in a variety of ways over your lifetime. Those values may vary according to individual characteristics and circumstances, but most groups of people hold some values in common. Knowing what some of those values are will help you find common ground with coworkers and others, even when you are not always in agreement over a particular issue.

As with the descriptions and definitions of leaders and leadership, there is a variety of perspectives about the most important values for leaders and the most important values in the leadership process. These are some of the values found in great leaders and in great leadership throughout time and across many cultures and continents:

- Purpose (a sense of importance)
- Truth
- Justice
- Empathy
- Empowerment (distributing power among others)
- Harmony with others

- Power *with*, not power *over*, others

- Just words and actions

- Sharing leadership with others

- Discipline

- Caring

- Understanding

- Awareness

- Celebration

- Imagination

- Perception

- Listening

- Openness

- Honesty

- Quality control

- Acceptance

- Fairness

ASK YOURSELF

Make a list of your most important values. Where did your values come from? How did they develop? Describe a leadership situation in which you were involved and explain what role each of these values played. Was the situation positive or negative? Why?

How do your three most important values affect how you teach children and the kind of environment you create for them?

Shared Values

A new perspective on values that focuses on the leader's relationship with followers has emerged in recent years. More and more, the literature on leadership reflects the concept of shared values rather than the leader's values. Shared values are the beliefs and ideals held in common by the individual and the group. Shared values are the means by which a group of people will achieve their goals and their mission. For leaders, sharing values means that no one person's values take priority, not even the leader's. The workplace will primarily reflect the top two or three values that everyone agrees to.

Values such as openness, caring, empowerment, listening, understanding, acceptance, and empathy are indicative of leaders who work in harmony with the needs and desires of other group members. Shared values change groups and organizations by doing the following:

- Fostering strong feelings of personal effectiveness
- Promoting high levels of group loyalty
- Facilitating consensus about key group goals and stakeholders
- Encouraging ethical behavior
- Promoting strong agreements about working hard and caring
- Reducing levels of job stress and tension

The idea of shared values encourages us to respond positively to one another, even when we do not always agree. You and another teacher may disagree on how much the children should be allowed to play with their food during lunch, but if you both share the value of children having nutritious food and keeping mealtimes pleasant, the two of you may decide to reach an agreement by alternating fun foods with opportunities to teach the children a variety of table manners. Sharing values between leaders and followers is a practice in two-way communicating that facilitates a stronger community and a commitment to the welfare of the community.

Ask Yourself

What values do you share with your coworkers? What specific shared goals can you accomplish by focusing on these shared values?

Having shared values does not mean that only one set of values exists. Pluralism and diversity are indispensable if we want true commitments to the common good of society. Shared values are a fundamental part of leadership in cultures and countries on every continent. Without some shared values, we would have a difficult time holding a group together during times of struggle, challenge, or disagreement. Without some differing values as well, we would have trouble coming up with innovative solutions or looking at problems from different angles.

For example, if you run a family child care program that serves children from more than one religious background, you and the parents may not always agree on what daily activities are appropriate for the children such as prayers before meals, food preparation, and fasting. However, if all the adults can agree that the children should feel good about themselves and should have experiences that teach them about their connectedness to others and how to treat each other with respect, you will all be more willing to continue working through the daily activities for the sake of holding the community together.

VISION

Vision is another important aspect of leadership. Visions are idealistic, distinctive, and unique, and they may differ from the current state of affairs. "Creating a vision," "the visible future," and "envisioning the future" are all phrases that refer to your ability to think long-term and imagine what lies ahead or what could lie ahead. When you have a vision, you are able to see the bigger picture and to imagine a better set of circumstances. A strong vision provides a focus for group members and encourages cooperation.

A good vision has six attributes:

- Future orientation

- Image

- Idealism

- Uniqueness

- Relevance

- A collective vision

Future Orientation

A sound vision must be future oriented. A vision represents a destination or a goal; the point in time of that destination is not important. A family child care provider may start children working on a collective mural that will be four days in the making. A preschool teacher may spend a month preparing a peace-and-justice classroom-management plan and not see the impact on children until the end of the year. A neighborhood group may spend three years implementing its vision of a school-age program that meets the needs of the community. A family may envision a new early learning center that will take a decade to reach its peak. The common thread in all these situations is future orientation—a vision of something that does not yet exist.

Image

Image is the second important attribute of a good vision. Good leaders are like good coaches. All coaches basically do the same things, but the good ones know what they want and can see how to get there. The same applies to good leaders. Good leaders not only realize that a better situation is possible; they have an image of what it looks like and how to get there. A good vision is clear about what will be involved in making the vision a reality. Your early childhood program may be considering accreditation as part of its vision for the future. Your role in the leadership process would be to clearly describe an accredited program using words and pictures that show your colleagues what the process would look like, how you would accomplish it, and how the program would be different when finished.

ASK YOURSELF

What is your vision of your work with children five years from now? How would you go about getting there? What values would you use to guide yourself? Why?

Think about the vision of your work with children five years from now and explain what that vision looks like. What words would you use to describe the better place you have envisioned? What would the children you serve be like? What relationship would you have with coworkers and families?

Idealism

A good vision is idealistic. It must be possible yet challenging. It may greatly improve on the current state of affairs or create a new one, but it should not be too easy to achieve. If it is too easy, there is a good possibility that someone else is already doing it. Leaders, at their personal best, engage in possibility thinking, the *What if? factor*. What if? is another way to structure your reflection. Describe what you would do for each What if? question that follows. What would each mean for you, for children, for families, for your community or society at large?

- What if you could restructure your work environment?

- What if you had all the money you needed to operate the program you wanted?

- What if you could change the early childhood education system?

- What if all children grew up to be just like you?

- What if no children grew up to be just like you?

Uniqueness

Uniqueness is the fourth attribute of a good vision. Leaders with a good vision strive to be different and take pride in that difference. A unique vision is what sets good leaders apart from everyone else—they provide something many want but few currently provide. This uniqueness creates pride within the group or organization because members take part in creating or producing something new, valuable, and important. The new specific-focus or theme-based centers coming into popularity are examples of organizations with unique visions. Centers now specialize in serving children with special needs, having extended hours of operation, and focusing on music and the arts. Each of these examples meets unique needs.

Relevance

A good vision must be relevant to those involved. Effective leaders know that a good vision is a reflection of group values and involves all group members. A relevant vision should improve the current situation and be challenging to achieve but also should be linked to the overall strategic direction of the group. For example, you may have a vision of the children you serve becoming bilingual in English and Mandarin, a goal to be achieved by all staff members becoming bilingual. This would be a challenging vision yet very meaningful in today's global society. However, if most of the children come from families that speak Vietnamese, the vision would be more relevant if everyone became bilingual in English and Vietnamese.

Ask Yourself

How is your vision different from what is happening now in your organization? Why is it different?

How does your vision include the visions of your coworkers? Of the children you serve? Of their families and communities? How do you know?

A Collective Vision

Finally, a good vision must be collective. That is, it must be shared by group members. Although the vision may originate from the leader, it cannot be achieved unless the group is as committed as the leader. It may be a wonderful vision to expose children to technology by having a computer or two in your classrooms, but the individual teacher must actually make it happen each day. The effective leader is able to communicate her vision in a way that attracts and commits others. Here are some strategies for creating a collective vision:

- Use a lot of images and word pictures
- Appeal to common beliefs
- Know your audience
- Include everybody—for example, different cultural groups, all ages and genders, major religions
- Say the same things in different ways
- Spend more time using words like *we* and *us* than *me* or *I*
- Be personally convinced that your vision is possible

These are all ways to communicate your vision to a group of people and win their enthusiasm and commitment. A collective vision changes people's relationship to the program. It is no longer *their* program; it becomes *our* program. Collective visions and values take you from *I* to *we* and from *theirs* to *ours*.

ASK YOURSELF

: **How does or how will your vision inspire others so they**
: **want to join you and be a part of what you want to create?**
: **How will you move your group from *I* to *we*?**

Vision is always important, whether you are the head of a family, the director of your own family child care or school-age care program, or the key organizer for a community-action group. Any leadership situation will require you to have a firm idea of where your group is going and what it will be like when you get there.

Communication, Social, and Interpersonal Skills

An effective leader works well with other people. Having productive working relationships begins with the open attitude we explored in the section on culture, but it doesn't end there. A leader also must get along well with people, whether or not he agrees with them, and communicate clearly. What good is a clear vision and strong values for you, or the area in which you are practicing leadership, if you cannot communicate them effectively to others?

COMMUNICATION SKILLS

Leadership requires the ability to communicate and explain what is happening in your environment. The first recognition of a person's leadership potential is often through her verbal skills. Early childhood education employees with strong verbal skills tend to have more organizational skills in the work setting and are able to rally coworkers. They do not simply repeat what the director or manager says but synthesize these views and their own.

An effective communicator

- Listens well

- Is listened to by others and sought out for advice

- Asks questions

- Comes up with ideas relevant to issues under discussion

- Speaks well

- Is open to new ideas

- Has a sense of humor

As a leader, you must be able to express yourself in words and ways that invite others into the conversation and make them want to stay and truly listen. You must also be able to listen to and understand others. You do not have to agree with them, but effective leaders do understand what others are trying to communicate and why they feel as they do. Really listening is a difficult skill to master, but becoming an effective listener is a tremendous step toward good leadership and good followership. Consider these questions as you think about your own listening skills:

- How comfortable are you when communicating with other adults?

- Sometimes listening to others sparks so many ideas and thoughts that you can't wait to speak. How long can you listen to another person without speaking? How long do you want them to listen to you?

- The next time you are in a casual conversation with someone, practice your listening skills. Make a list of the other person's main points and ask if what you wrote is what they meant to convey.

ASK YOURSELF

Have someone whose opinion you value and trust observe you for a couple of days and make notes about your communication with children and adults. What do you think of the observation? How will you use the information?

> **Do you use a different set of communication skills with children than you do with adults? Why do you think this is so?**

SOCIAL SKILLS

Social skills are another sign of your leadership potential. You use them to get along with people, and others use them to get along with you. Those people with strong social skills can easily get involved with groups inside and outside of the center. Strong social skills are a necessary part of team building and collaboration, which we will discuss later. You have strong social skills if you

- Like people and make friends easily

- Are honest and build trust easily

- Are warm and outgoing

- Are not afraid to get to know a group of people

- Let others take credit

- Are flexible

- Have a sense of your own identity

- Are self-directed

- Interact with others in a positive manner

- Have a sense of humor

As you begin to increase your communication and social skills, take some of your cues from children. As adults, we lose some of our unself-conscious ability to connect with people. When children who don't know each other meet, you'll often hear something such as "I have one of those at home" or "What grade are you in?" Adults feel more self-conscious and awkward. Sometimes the best we can manage is "Nice weather." Children say things that encourage conversation and dialogue. They want an authentic response. Sometimes we grown-ups want to pretend we've had a conversation when we really haven't and really do not want to. We've all been in situations in which "How are you?" is only a rhetorical question.

INTERPERSONAL SKILLS

Strong verbal and social skills come together to create another important tool in effective leadership: strong interpersonal communication. Interpersonal communication involves these abilities:

- Sensing group attitudes, motives, and feelings, and addressing these to the satisfaction of group members—for example, when a new licensing requirement is under discussion, you can tell that most of the group is opposed, even if they don't all say so out loud

- Sensing the needs of others and responding in a variety of ways, depending on the situation—for example, when explaining a new activity you want to try to coworkers, you can tell some people need a different kind of explanation

- Determining what is really happening in an interaction, why people are behaving in certain ways, and what you can do about it—for example, when you are talking to a parent who isn't fluent in your language and she is nodding her head, you can tell she may not be understanding everything you say

- Really caring about others, getting to know them well enough to truly understand their viewpoint, and communicating effectively so they truly understand your viewpoint—for example, when you intentionally arrange a getting-to-know-you time with parents with no other agenda or business in mind

These interpersonal skills are essential for effective leadership because they will help you learn the needs of the group you are leading. Use the information to build an effective team. When you use these skills, you will spend more time listening to other people and paying attention to how they are responding to you. When you do not use these skills, people may feel that you are not really interested in what they think and how they feel. Opportunities for team building are lost because team members either have little motivation to implement your ideas or they are unclear about what your ideas actually are.

You can also use these interpersonal communication skills to learn more about how culture influences people's communication and interaction patterns. As you begin to spend more time with people who are culturally different from you, you will increase your ability to notice and interpret cultural differences in body language and learn to adjust your own verbal and physical communication patterns. When coworkers whose native language is not English are trying to communicate, effective leaders listen carefully. Effective leaders ask questions and learn about how different people approach conflicts and disagreements. Your coworkers will recognize a familiar approach when you take it, they will notice that you use many different styles and patterns of communication and interaction, and they will feel more like part of a real team. They will be more open with you and listen more carefully to your perspectives and your ways of seeing the world. Good interpersonal skills beget better interpersonal skills.

Summary

Effective leaders understand that cultural differences influence how each of us makes sense of the world and how we approach a leadership situation or opportunity. In this chapter, you've been challenged to think more about the values and the vision that define where you want to go and how you intend to get there. Reflection on your communication skills has given you the opportunity to increase and improve your interactions with others. Chapter 4 looks at leadership at every level of the early childhood education field and examines how you can increase your collaboration and team-building skills with families and communities.

STORY TIME

John really wanted to work more collaboratively with his new team teacher, Mehret. He told her that the two of them should meet weekly to talk about their goals for the children. Mehret liked the idea, so John enthusiastically scheduled their meetings and gave her a list of agenda items they could cover. The list included a number of exciting ideas John liked from a workshop he and Mehret had attended that summer; he was looking forward to implementing them.

The meetings seemed to be going well—kind of. Something was not quite right, but John couldn't put his finger on it. Mehret met with him regularly, as scheduled, and she listened politely to all of his ideas and seemed to be quite agreeable. Still, their team teaching did not seem as smooth as it should have been, and Mehret often caught him off guard by adding pieces they had not discussed or by making unexpected changes. John thought the additions were good; they just caught him off guard.

At a workshop the next month, John told the trainer about his situation. After getting some additional information and listening carefully to how John described his experience, she asked him, "What is Mehret doing and saying during your meetings?" John realized that in his enthusiasm and excitement, he had not paid much attention to what Mehret was doing. She always smiled, but she never said much. John thought about that for a while.

When John got to work the next day, he told Mehret that he realized he hadn't included her in planning their weekly agenda and had unfortunately assumed that she liked his ideas because she hadn't said otherwise. Mehret then explained to him that he was always so excited about his own ideas that he never really created enough space in his conversation for her to talk about her own exciting ideas, so she just added them into their curriculum where she could. They agreed that they would take turns planning the meetings and sharing ideas so they could increase their ability to listen to each other, understand each other's viewpoint, and combine them to make the curriculum as exciting for the children as it was for the two of them.

More Reading

Bolman, Lee G., and Terrence E. Deal. 1997. *Reframing organizations: Artistry, choice, and leadership.* San Francisco: Jossey-Bass.

Bruno, Holly Elissa. 2009. *Leading on purpose: Emotionally intelligent early childhood administration.* Boston: McGraw-Hill Higher Education.

Chang, Hedy Nai-Lin, Amy Muckelroy, and Dora Pulido-Tobiassen. 1996. *Looking in, looking out: Redefining child care and early education in a diverse society.* Ed. Carol Dowell. Oakland: California Tomorrow.

Cohen, Allan R., and David L. Bradford. 1991. *Influence without authority.* New York: John Wiley.

Gentile, Mary C., ed. 1994. *Differences that work: Organizational excellence through diversity.* Boston: Harvard Business School Press.

Gonzalez-Mena, Janet. 2008. *Diversity in early care and education: Honoring differences.* 5th ed. Boston: McGraw-Hill Higher Education.

———. 1993. *Multicultural issues in child care.* Mountain View, CA: Mayfield.

Jalongo, Mary Renck. 2008. *Learning to listen, listening to learn: Building essential skills in young children.* Washington, DC: National Association for the Education of Young Children.

Kouzes, James M., and Barry Z. Posner. 1987. *The leadership challenge: How to get extraordinary things done in organizations.* San Francisco: Jossey-Bass.

Mallory, Bruce L., and Rebecca S. New, eds. 1994. *Diversity and developmentally appropriate practices: Challenges for early childhood education.* New York: Teachers College Press.

Moore, Thomas. 2003. Bringing diversity into your center. In *The art of leadership: Managing early childhood organizations.* Rev. ed. Eds. Bonnie Neugebauer and Roger Neugebauer, 364–66. Redmond, WA: Child Care Information Exchange.

Neugebauer, Bonnie, ed. 1992. *Alike and different: Exploring our humanity with young children.* Washington, DC: National Association for the Education of Young Children.

Ramirez III, Manuel, and Alfredo Castaneda. 1974. *Cultural democracy, bicognitive development, and education.* New York: Academic Press.

Samovar, Larry A., and Richard E. Porter, eds. 1997. *Intercultural communication: A reader.* 8th ed. Boston: Wadsworth.

Thompson, Becky, and Sangeeta Tyagi, eds. 1996. *Names we call home: Autobiography on racial identity.* New York: Routledge.

Three Rivers, Amoja. 1991. *Cultural etiquette: A guide for the well-intentioned.* Indian Valley, VA: Market Wimmin.

Wheatley, Margaret J. 1994. *Leadership and the new science: Learning about organization from an orderly universe.* San Francisco: Berrett-Koehler.

Chapter 4

▲

It Takes a Village

It takes a village to raise a child—we've all heard that. But what does it take to create a village? In a village, every grown-up has a valued, understood role in the education, health, welfare, growth, and development of the children who live there. All of the grown-ups understand this, and all of the children take it for granted. If you want to influence the lives of children and their families or influence the status and cohesiveness of the profession of early childhood education in the United States, it does not matter what level within the field you currently occupy—we're all villagers. We can all be advocates and leaders, regardless of our roles. We each have a valued and essential role in creating the village that will raise all of our children.

In early childhood care and education, we are still working to create that village for children and to understand and value each of our roles in raising America's children. Leadership at all levels of early childhood education programs has a key part in leadership at local, national, and international levels. This chapter looks at how each of us has a role in creating that village for the children, their families, and our profession. Effective communicating, storytelling, team building, collaborating with families, and advocating are ways to practice leadership at all levels in our field and increase our cohesiveness and our connections to each other.

Leadership at Every Level

The strength and enthusiasm of leadership at the middle and lower levels of any group or program create the strength and enthusiasm at the top.

For a program to do its best for children and families, leadership must be present at all levels in every early childhood care and education setting, whether that be a family child care home, a center, a school-age care program, or a preschool. Leaderlike actions and qualities must come from every teacher, assistant, aide, and support staff member—every adult. We need to recognize the leadership ability we bring to our own circles of influence—to the people we interact with on a regular basis—and begin to make connections between this leadership ability and the ability to influence what happens in our lives and in the lives of children. Leadership does not occur only at the top levels, and it is not always the sole property of the person in charge. In practice, it is spread throughout all levels, and this distribution is essential for a healthy system. Everyone in every program or organization must be ready to take leaderlike action so each level can function effectively.

Leadership builds on itself. Many of the best leaders in almost any field have come up through the ranks. Very few people develop leadership skills suddenly. The leadership talents of some may be well hidden for years, but with patience, practice, reflection, and the right circumstances, leadership talent will develop and emerge. For example, Barbara Bowman, founder of the Erikson Institute, a graduate school and research center in Chicago that focuses on child development, began her career as a classroom teacher.

Unfortunately, many people imagine that leadership skills like team building, collaboration, and advocacy belong only to professors, lobbyists, and leaders of large professional organizations. Too many people see leadership as something they can never attain. This kind of thinking is not only untrue, it seriously inhibits our ability to mobilize the early childhood education profession and draw on each of our unique strengths and skills. Any team building, collaboration, or advocacy—any leadership—at any level adds to our power and to our ability to turn things around. The only tools we need are actions and words. To assert leadership, you have to say something to or do something with someone else, and you have to tell others that you are doing it. Here are some ways to get started:

- Pick an issue or topic that generates strong feelings for you, and find out more about it. Link your issue or topic to a larger group of people, like a community organization. Decide what you will say or do to present the topic to others. Then get going.

- Leadership at all levels means taking action or speaking up wherever you find yourself and wherever you are needed. How do you take action? When do you speak up or speak out?

- Leaders and advocates take action on their good ideas. How do you take action on your good ideas? How long does it usually take you to move from idea to action?

- Arrange times to interview leaders at different levels. How did each person develop their leadership skills and abilities? What challenges have made them who they are today? Who influences them? What makes them unique?

- Arrange times for others to observe and interview you. What do they notice about what you do? Do their observations match your image of yourself as a leader? What can you tell them about your own leadership development?

Team Building

Team building is essential if everyone in an organization is going to be a leader some of the time. Team building in early childhood care and education happens when you create processes, interactions, and activities that help a group of people become an effective and efficient team that meets the needs of the children and families you serve, as well as those of your organization as a whole. Team building gathers all the people who work in your program—the cook, the driver, the receptionist, and the custodian as well as teachers, assistants, and aides—so everyone has an opportunity to see their roles in working toward the common goal or vision.

Most early childhood education programs already use some team-building activities, such as bringing teachers together to think about programming and curriculum or to learn new skills; holding a potluck, picnic, or dinner event together; having "secret pals" in larger programs;

or exchanging gifts during holiday seasons. The best way to build teams is to have every adult who is part of the organization participate in some way. Remember what we said about every person taking leaderlike action so the organization works well? For this to happen, everyone in the organization has to be seen as part of the team. For example, custodians contribute to children's learning when they take responsibility for discipline, playground supervision, and modeling appropriate responses to disagreements and conflicts.

Team building is also a way to strengthen collaboration with your colleagues. It is a way to begin recognizing how each role adds to the leadership the children see in your environment. For example, in my daughter's preschool program, Miss F, the cook, was just as important in her daily life as Miss D, her teacher. Every day, my daughter would come home with a story about what Miss F said or did or what Miss F knew about each child's eating preferences. You can start team building by thinking about who the team is right now and what each person brings to it.

Ask Yourself

On a sports team, each player has a different role and brings a different strength to the team effort. Make a list of every adult in your program. What is the number one strength or gift each person adds to the team? What would the team and the children be lacking if that person was not there to bring that strength or gift?

What is your relationship with each of the adults in your program? Do you have regular conversations about what each of you wants for the children or the families served? If not, ask what each person wants most for the children and their families.

What is each adult's relationship with the children? You can learn a lot about who the children think is part of the team by observing their interactions with the other adults

> in the environment. Ask each adult if she feels like she's a
> part of the team. If yes, ask why. If no, ask why not.
>
> Are there support staff in your program? Are they invited
> to regular program meetings and do they participate? If
> they are not part of program meetings, you can suggest
> that they be invited.

In your role as a leader, you have daily opportunities to talk with your team members. You play a part in recognizing that everyone is on the team and acknowledging that leadership takes place on every level in your work setting. You will begin to think differently about your interactions with coworkers, and you will add to the overall team building in your program.

Collaboration with Families

It is impossible to raise a child in any village that does not involve that child's family! Joining forces and resources with families will strengthen your ability to provide children with what they need to reach their full potential. Family and parent involvement focuses on the importance of parents and families in the care and education of their children. (Books to help increase and enhance collaboration with parents and families are listed at the end of this chapter.) Families should serve in an ongoing and highly visible capacity in centers, schools, and other early child care settings.

Working with families also will strengthen your leadership ability. Working with families is different from working with colleagues. They play a different role in the lives of their children than staff do, and they have different concerns about children's well-being. They also may come from a different background than you do—for example, a different culture, class, or language. Learning to balance these things while you uncover your shared values and your shared vision for the children is the essence of leadership.

The strongest form of collaboration with families is, of course, making sure they have equal voice and equal say in the decision-making process. This collaboration must be more than just a legal formality or a token gesture. Parents want to feel accepted and encouraged to participate in meetings and activities. Few parents become involved if the focus is on parents' shortcomings or if staff assume that parents cannot be experts on their own children's strengths and challenges. When parents participate equally with the early childhood professionals who care for and teach their children, their self-esteem increases; they will begin to enjoy participating as members of a productive group. You will also have a stronger, more meaningful relationship with parents and families if they feel they are working with you on behalf of the children.

ASK YOURSELF

What is your relationship with the adult family members of the children you serve? Do you have regular conversations with each of them about what they want for their children? If not, ask each person what he wants most for the children.

GETTING TO KNOW FAMILIES

You can take a variety of collaborative steps with parents to strengthen children's abilities and increase parents' participation in the leadership process. You can begin a relationship by simply finding out more about each other. Select a family you have not spent much time with, and just focus on getting to know them better as people. What are their interests? Hobbies? What foods do they like best? These little things can serve as bridges to conversations about bigger things, such as goals for children.

When you have moved beyond the initial discomfort of speaking with a family you don't know very well, you can ask parents and family members if they have a goal you can work on collaboratively for the child this year. For example, a couple of parents may want their children to retain their home language. You could label or name a few items in more than one language throughout your program as a way to reinforce home language. Begin by letting parents and other adult family members choose the focus of your collaborating efforts. By letting them go first, you are demonstrating that you want an equal collaboration, that you respect their role as their children's first teachers, and that the collaboration will be beneficial to them. You are giving them some control—an essential component of facilitative leadership.

As you increase your collaboration with families, they will begin to increase their relationship with you and will be more open to collaborating on a goal you select—for example, parental/family support in helping a young child use words to express her feelings. It will become increasingly easier for you to work together as a team for the best interest of their child. You will be able to join your forces and resources, recognizing that each of you holds important information about who the child is and what she needs. The kind of collaboration you learn by working with parents and families will transfer to other areas within the profession and to other areas of your life as well.

GETTING TO KNOW THE SURROUNDING COMMUNITY

You can increase your leadership skills by extending your collaboration with families to include the surrounding community. You don't have to be the head of your program to begin collaborating with the community. Getting to know more about it is another way to practice leadership at all levels. For all children to be successful, we must foster new relationships among the children, teachers, parents, and the community—we must create the village. The first step is to find out more about the community you serve and the relationship you and your program have with it.

ASK YOURSELF

Find out what neighborhoods and communities your program serves. Where do the children live? Do community children attend your program? Do you know why or why not?

What elementary schools are in the community? Do the children you serve attend more than one? Get to know the kindergarten and first-grade teachers. Invite them to visit your classroom or home program; then visit theirs. In June, have a potluck with parents of children you serve and invite the kindergarten and first-grade teachers who will have the children next year.

Study the community's history. If the families you serve live in the community where your program is located, ask them about the community's history. Has it changed over the years? Is the population growing older or younger? Reflect on what the answers mean for your program.

How many community organizations are in the neighborhood you serve? Make a list of them, and then introduce yourself to the leaders of each. Let the organizations know you teach children in the community, and ask for information about each one's mission and services. Check out such organizations as the Urban League and the Boys and Girls Clubs of America. What do they do? Ask them if there are ways you can work together.

Does your program have an advisory group or board of directors? If not, use the information you've gathered from the community to make suggestions for a new advisory group or board of directors. Be sure that the members are also involved with some of the community groups and organizations.

These activities will increase your collaboration skills, make you more knowledgeable about the community you work in, and enhance your role as a member of your work team. At the same time, you will increase your leadership ability. Collaborating with children's communities is such an important topic that we will cover it in more detail in the next chapter.

Advocacy

Leadership in advocacy involves building bridges between early childhood care and education settings and the communities we serve. All of the issues we face go beyond our work and into the homes and the communities of the children. By finding the links among professional, home, and community issues, we can identify starting points for advocacy. Advocates share their knowledge with others, going beyond good intentions and acting on what they know. Here are some first steps you can take to stretch your leadership wings in the area of advocacy:

- Start a parent teacher association (PTA) for your program if one has not been established.

- Find out where various political candidates stand on issues involving children, and vote responsibly.

- Tell parents, friends, and neighbors how you intend to vote and why.

- Pick two or three highlights from a report on the connection between wages and program quality in early care and education, and share them with every adult you meet.

- Find out whether the butcher, the baker, and the candlestick maker in your community have children, grandchildren, nieces, or nephews. Strike up a conversation about the children they care for and how they are affected by public policy.

- Speak at a conference on how you are developing your leadership and advocacy roles within the field.

- If you are not comfortable making a presentation at a conference, make arrangements to host an informal conversation on a hot topic at your table during lunch.

- Contact elementary schools and community organizations; find out what issues you have in common.

- Always be prepared to explain what you do with children and why.

- Support your colleagues in getting more training and education, and support accreditation for your workplace.

- If you are not ready to give a testimony at a public hearing, go to support someone who is.

- If you are already an actively engaged advocate, mentor someone else to become an advocate.

Leadership in creating a village means finding the *yes* and the *how* in advocacy, not the *why I can't*. Opportunities for advocacy, like opportunities for all leadership, are presented to us many times a day. Always ask yourself what you can do right now to turn the current situation into an opportunity to speak up or take action on behalf of children, families, and our profession.

Leadership requires the ability to articulate your program's mission, goals, and purpose in ways that others can understand. Your best voice may come from telling stories. In every village there is a storyteller—a person who explains the past, interprets the present, and predicts the future through stories. When you tell a story, you bring bits of information to life. Storytelling is certainly no stranger to most early childhood education teachers!

Ask Yourself

In what ways do you talk about child development theory to parents and others in the community? What do you say about what you do and how you influence children's growth and development?

What stories can you tell in your own little circle of influence that can spread out to increasingly large audiences?

Have you told the parents a story about how pretend and symbolic play create the foundation for future reading skills? This would be an excellent way to advocate for developmentally appropriate activities for children.

Listen to the stories told by others in your work environment. What do they tell you? What do you think they mean? When you retell the stories, how do you explain what they mean?

So many stories can be shared with so many people in so many places. Don't be apologetic while telling a good story. We early childhood educators must become more courageous in standing up for ourselves. The stories we tell are true, and we hold the key to how the story will eventually end. We know that things like higher wages, funding for training, support services for families, and child-friendly legislation increase the quality of what we do, and we should not apologize for advocating them. Leadership requires our strong voices. Children require our strong voices. No matter how small you think your voice is, it is bigger and stronger and louder than most children's voices.

Summary

To help create a village, you can use advocacy, storytelling, effective communication, team building, and collaboration with families and communities. Many of these techniques are already familiar to you from the work you do with children, other staff members, and families every day. These activities provide abundant opportunities for people at every level of early childhood care and education to lead the way toward better programs, more effective organizations, and brighter futures for children. Whatever your position in your program, you are a leader in creating a village that can care for all children. In chapter 5, we will take a closer look at how you can continue to create the village by collaborating with community organizations, building coalitions, and strengthening community leadership through your work with young children.

STORY TIME

Zakiya was preparing for Merrilee's performance-evaluation meeting. Merrilee had been the receptionist at Zakiya's Village Preschool for a month. Her primary job was to answer phones and greet families and others who came in to the school. Zakiya's Village Preschool's mission was to provide children with a village-like environment where all grown-ups had a valued role in the education and development of the village's children. Merrilee was young, enthusiastic, and new to the world of work. She liked Zakiya's Village Preschool and felt she had a great relationship with her supervisor. Zakiya had supported her professional development from the very beginning. Merrilee went into Zakiya's office feeling a little nervous, since this was her first performance review, but she was confident that she had been doing a good job. Zakiya had a set of performance factors that she used for all of Zakiya's Village Preschool staff: job knowledge, quality of performance, creating the village (team building), and making the mission happen.

The meeting was going well. Merrilee was knowledgeable about the rates and hours of Zakiya's Village Preschool and the qualifications of the teachers. Her professionalism and efficiency in answering phones and providing information were good indicators of the quality of her performance. Merrilee was also an active participant in all-staff team-building activities.

Finally, they approached the last factor in the evaluation. "So tell me, Merrilee," Zakiya said. "How does your work support our mission to provide children with a village-like environment?" "It doesn't," replied Merrilee. Zakiya was surprised. "Tell me more about that." "Well," continued Merrilee, "I'm just the receptionist. I'm not a teacher. My work doesn't have anything to do with the mission." Zakiya pondered this for a while and decided to take an unconventional approach. "Well, I guess that means you can't work here," she said with a smile. Now it was Merrilee's turn to be surprised. She looked shocked, so Zakiya quickly put her at ease. "Relax, Merrilee. You're doing a great job. As you know, part of our mission is to recognize that every grown-up has a valued role in our children's village. In a village, leadership is required at all levels. You are not 'just a receptionist.' For the public, our families, and our children, you are the first face they see, the first voice they hear. To many people, you *are* Zakiya's Village Preschool."

Merrilee left her performance review feeling great; more importantly, she left feeling valued and important. She had not thought of herself as a leader before and had never thought about her leadership role. She returned to her desk with a new sense of confidence in her ability to have a positive impact on her workplace and the children.

More Reading

Bruno, Holly Elissa. 2009. *Leading on purpose: Emotionally intelligent early childhood administration*. Boston: McGraw-Hill Higher Education.

Etzioni, Amitai. 1991. *A responsive society: Collected essays on guiding deliberate social change*. San Francisco: Jossey-Bass.

Ghiselin, Bernie. 1990. *Forging consensus: Building a dialogue among diverse leaders*. Special report. Greensboro, NC: Center for Creative Leadership.

Gonzalez-Mena, Janet. 2008. *Diversity in early care and education: Honoring differences*. 5th ed. Boston: McGraw-Hill Higher Education.

Kahn, Si. 1991. *Organizing: A guide for grassroots leaders*. Washington, DC: National Association of Social Workers.

Kaner, Sam. 1996. *Facilitator's guide to participatory decision-making*. Gabriola Island, British Columbia: New Society, Limited.

Mattessich, Paul W., and Barbara R. Monsey. 1992. *Collaboration—What makes it work: A review of research literature on factors influencing successful collaboration*. St. Paul, MN: Amherst H. Wilder Foundation.

McCaleb, Sudia Paloma. 1997. *Building communities of learners: A collaboration among teachers, students, families, and communities*. Mahwah, NJ: Lawrence Erlbaum Associates.

Stonehouse, Anne. 1995. *How does it feel? Child care from a parent's perspective*. Redmond, WA: Child Care Information Exchange.

Wynn, Mychal. 2005. *Empowering African-American males: A guide to increasing Black male achievement*. Ed. Glenn Bascome. Marietta, GA: Rising Sun.

Zander, Alvin. 1990. *Effective social action by community groups*. San Francisco: Jossey-Bass.

Chapter 5

▲

Leadership Connections with Schools and Communities

In chapter 4, I talked about creating the village needed to raise children. The communities we live in are the villages that must support children, and a major village institution in any community is the school. This chapter will focus on how to make and strengthen connections between your program, schools, and communities and on opportunities for leadership development in programs that serve young children when they are not in school. You will learn about community leadership and social action and how to form collaborative relationships with community organizations, work with a very diverse group, assess a community's needs for its children, and apply effective strategies to achieve community goals.

When young children turn five, they go to school, but not all day and not all year. School-age care is a critical piece of the early childhood field, and programs that serve young school children have an important role in your leadership development and your leadership role in bringing children and adults together in meaningful ways. You have great opportunities to create a place where families spend time together and great opportunities to really get to know a child's community!

School-age care is the term that covers most of the programs set up to serve children when they are not in school. This includes before- and after-school programs, spring- and winter-break programs, and a variety of summer programs. Although school-age programs serve children ages five to thirteen, the focus here will be on the early years, children up to age eight.

We all know that early childhood doesn't end when a child starts kindergarten, and many communities in the United States have changed considerably from the time when they felt children were safe just hanging around outdoors during summer and other school breaks. It is very important to provide high-quality programs in which young school children are safe, have fun, learn social skills, and learn to accept and respect one another. Family and community members really appreciate the fact that good programs assist in supervising and developing children when they are not in school.

Often we think of early childhood programs as primarily serving children, but in fact programs serving school-age children have four clients: children, parents, sponsors, and the community. Sponsors could be a school, the parks department, a community agency, a business, a church or temple, or some other agency or organization, such as Rotary Boys and Girls Clubs, the Urban League, and the YMCA or YWCA. Many programs are cosponsored by two or more different groups. Cosponsored programs have many advantages because each group contributes its strengths, skills, abilities, and constituents. A group with an established track record in child care for young school children can offer another group its great expertise in running the complicated and time-consuming details of a program. One example is a Seattle, Washington, public elementary school that added a preschool program. The school partnered with the local YMCA, which has a strong history of serving children, to offer child care programs at the school during school breaks and before and after school.

Ask Yourself

Young children may spend many hours in your care, but they are still members of their communities. What do you want your role to be in growing good citizens for diverse communities?

Many programs that serve young school children have a mission or a vision that mentions connections to community. What is unique about your program compared to other active groups in the community?

How would you describe your program's role in serving the community and its children? How would you describe your responsibility to the community whose children you serve?

What are some of your personal and professional goals in your work with children and their families? What do you want to accomplish? What is important to you in your work?

Community Leadership and Social Action

Programs that serve young school children can help children learn more about cultural differences and their roles in individual communities and society at large. So what is a community? A community is a group of people with something in common, or something shared:

- A location or geographical area, such as a neighborhood

- A culture or set of values, such as the Lummi Nation

- A language, such as Amharic

- A race, such as European American

- An ethnicity, such as Greek

- A religious belief, such as Baha'i

- A set of political beliefs, such as the Green Party's

- A historical event, such as enslavement or the Holocaust

- A set of shared practices, such as vegetarianism

- A physical ability, such as that of the Deaf and hearing-impaired community

- An occupation, such as farming

Communities link and connect us in ways that allow us to identify ourselves and allow others to recognize us as part of a particular community. The strength of a community comes in the relationships members have with each other—relationships that are the foundation of working together for change. Children are future beneficiaries and leaders of our many communities, and the ways early childhood programs help strengthen communities have great impacts on the health of the communities they will inherit.

Community leadership refers to those actions carried out by individuals or groups that affect events and activities in neighborhoods, towns, and specific groups of people. It usually involves the use of influence, power, and information in decision-making. It is very complex and very diverse.

Community leadership can result from one person taking on an activity that attracts the attention of others. Most people can recall the activities of a single individual who set out to change or improve herself, a community organization, or the conditions of a group. For example, many of us are familiar with the efforts of John Woolman, a Quaker in the mid-1700s, who almost single-handedly eliminated the practice of enslaving African Americans among members of the Society of Friends. He accomplished this by asking the Friends, one person at a time, how the enslavement of others affected them as moral people.

Community leadership can also be a grassroots effort. A recent example is the way President Barack Obama engaged large numbers of young voters in his bid for the presidency; he rallied young people by using the technology, tools, strategies, and patterns that young people use to communicate with each other. The result was the election of the first African American as President of the United States. Another historical example is that of Queen Liliuokalani, the first queen and last reigning monarch of Hawai'i at the turn of the nineteenth century. Liliuokalani became queen at the age of fifty-two, when her brother Kalākaua passed away. Prior to that, she had worked behind the scenes, using her strong will and commitment to the islands to influence the actions of her brother and keep Hawai'i from being annexed by the United States. Although Liliuokalani was by no means an everyday person, it is important for us to remember that many women have had a strong influence in local and world events without the cloak of formal leadership authority.

Community leadership can also result from a group of people trying to bring about a change in their community. An example of this is provided by John White in his discussion (1990) of the grassroots activities of local churches and community members to support Black national leaders of the civil rights movement.

Another example of community leadership involves a coalition of smaller groups that combine their resources to achieve a goal. The Coalition for Equal Education Rights (CEER) in Seattle, Washington, is an example. CEER is comprised of a number of education, social change, and social service organizations, such as the Praxis Institute for Early Childhood Education, Tabor 100, and the Mockingbird Society. These groups have come together to address the academic achievement gap faced by local African American students. The goal of the coalition is to create and implement a strategic plan by combining the resources of all member organizations.

Why do ordinary people in a community engage in social action and change? Many leaders who volunteer their time, energy, and resources become involved for personal or social reasons. Often, social action is the result of strong dissatisfaction with what is happening in a community or society. Some people become active because they see a good that can be accomplished and feel personally rewarded by their own efforts to achieve it. People also become involved in community and social action because they feel it is the only way to obtain the voice and the power to solve problems. Alvin Zander (1990) believed that people often engage in community and social action for one or more of three motives:

- Some people have self-oriented motives and seek personal satisfaction, such as purity of the soul, excitement, admiration, power/influence, pride in achievement, and the elimination of tension or worry.

- Some people want to help their group or another group succeed, even if individual success is not possible.

- Some people become involved in community and social action because of a desire to improve conditions in the community or society at large.

In many cases, issues of powerlessness and empowerment arise. Too often, people feel dissatisfied by the way things are but feel that, individually, they can't do much to change the situation. Community creates a sense of ownership, responsibility, and belonging that pushes people beyond individual self-interest to understand the interrelationship between the community's health and their own well-being. One challenge is that many people have difficulty crossing or stepping outside rigid roles, such as teacher, parent, or city council member, to interact with each other as equal members of the same community. Relationships based primarily on familiar roles may be friendly and comfortable, but people in role-based relationships tend to focus on how community circumstances affect their own well-being and not the well-being of the community as a whole. It is almost impossible to make meaningful changes in a community under such conditions. To move outside of familiar-role relationships, people have to talk to each other as equals working on behalf of the community's health and well-being.

Ask Yourself

Think about your family while you were growing up. What were some of the ways members of your family were involved in community leadership or social action? Were there community meetings or neighborhood watch groups? Did family members join marches or protests? Did your family participate in providing services to others?

Think about yourself as a child. What were some of the ways you were involved in community leadership or social action? For example, were you careful not to litter? Did you stand up for another child? Did you participate in recycling or collect canned goods for a food drive?

Forming Collaborative Relationships with Community Organizations

Communities remain strong when everyone with a stake in children's development works together. You and your program enhance the quality of life in a community through your collaboration with community efforts. Through your community collaborations, you can play a part in empowering communities. Community leaders often emerge from working with a community organization like yours. When opportunities arise, many community members will be eager to assume leadership responsibilities that will improve their communities. Most community members want to work with community organizations, and your program is, by default, a community organization.

In chapter 1, we discussed three leadership functions:

- Transformational leadership, which seeks to change the leader and the follower into better people, better leaders

- Situational leadership, whose purpose changes as the leadership situation or needs change

- Servant leadership, which puts leaders in the position of serving others

In this chapter, we will add one more:

- Transactional leadership, in which leaders and followers, or co-leaders, exchange something of equal value or importance

Transactional Leadership

Transactional leadership has an important role in early childhood programs serving school-age children. Transactional leadership is a form of social exchange in which leaders and followers see each other as potential agents for meeting specific material, social, and psychological goals. Your involvement with and relationship to community members can begin with a simple exchange of mutual influence and support while both parties seek ways to grow stronger, achieve goals, and develop stronger, more powerful voices. With time, this relationship can develop into a powerful partnership that has the ability to influence other organizations, agencies, and even political outcomes. In transactional leadership, organizations work with each other without necessarily changing each other. In transformational leadership, organizations work with each other to renew and transform each other.

Building relationships within the community helps you create healthy, integrated environments for children and leads to increased support and collaboration. Your relationship to and communication with members of the community you serve must involve a genuine encounter. You are not just volunteering your own quality time. In a genuine encounter, you are getting something out of the relationship too: you are receiving quality time from community members as well. A genuine encounter is inherently mutual. Both participants give and take, contribute and consume, and talk and listen. True quality time is a mutually beneficial two-way street. In a community, people interact on a daily basis. Such relationships are based on shared values and shared interests; they can only occur when people are able to spend time getting to know each other through talking and finding common values and interests. Strong bonds and high levels of trust are created when community members spend time together at community activities, such as sporting events; church, synagogue, or temple functions; school, park, and social events; and other opportunities for authentic engagement. As a leader in collaborative, community-based efforts, you should keep the following guidelines in mind:

- Have high levels of expertise in the field

- Guide, organize, and present alternatives

- Empower the team by encouraging confidence and initiative in all members

- Serve as the visionary in the group

- Have patience for high levels of frustration

- Be politically astute

- Ensure that all views and opinions are equally welcomed and heard

- Demonstrate sensitivity and awareness of individuality

- Inspire commitment and action

- Sustain hope and inspiration

- Build broad-based involvement

- Enable social and financial diversification

- Set a tone that eliminates turf

- Promote relationships among participants that cross familiar role lines

- Ensure that all participants have opportunities to use all the gifts and talents they bring to the collaboration

Following these guidelines will help you form authentic relationships with community members and set the stage for creating healthy environments for children.

Ask Yourself

What is the current image of your organization in the local community? How do you know?

What is your relationship with the community being served by your program?

What are your coworkers' general opinions, perspectives, and perceptions about the communities you serve? How do you know?

Community Relationship Opportunities

Consider undertaking some of these initiatives to develop and enrich relationships between your school-age program and its community:

- Hold a community forum on programs for young school children, such as a speaker series, panels, workshops, or open discussion gatherings appropriate to your desired outcomes and the type of information you are presenting.

- Facilitate conversations between the community, a school, and an early childhood program serving school-age children.

- Find ways to make use of community spaces. Children have many developmental needs when it comes to space: open, outdoor space for loud and active play; space for mid-level noise for activities like board games and cards; quiet space appropriate for activities like reading, homework, and reflection. High-quality programs can maximize these needs through the use of various community facilities.

Most communities also offer opportunities to work with people who are diverse in a variety of ways—for example, in race, ethnicity, religion, language, political perspective, sexual orientation, economic level, and social/cultural perspective. The ability to work in diverse multicultural, multiracial, and multilingual groups is an essential skill needed for community and social action groups because our communities, and society in general, are becoming more diverse. The very nature of leadership requires potential leaders to develop a variety of approaches for collaborating and deciding on common or shared focuses. Effective leaders must have or develop skills in decision making and planning that incorporate competing viewpoints, agendas, and interests.

In his report *Forging Consensus: Building a Dialogue among Diverse Leaders*, Bernie Ghiselin (1990) describes the activities of a diverse group of community leaders who had to develop a bond package that a majority of the city's voters would support. The thirty-seven members of the Greensboro (North Carolina) One Task Force included representatives from the local Black university, the Rotary and Kiwanis clubs, the Junior League, the Chamber of Commerce, and neighborhood groups. Ten African Americans, ten women, and people from a number of socioeconomic levels attended the meetings. All thirty-seven members had been active in community affairs in one way or another. As you can see, this was an extremely diverse group.

Coming to an agreement when diverse needs and objectives are involved can be challenging and rewarding but can result in dynamic changes in a community. Children can learn a lot about their future roles in a community by seeing how a diverse group of adults can work together to solve problems, achieve goals, and change communities.

ASK YOURSELF

Communities today are very diverse. Who is the community is represented by the children in your program?

Who is most likely to join in an activity or action that builds community relationships?

NEEDS ASSESSMENT

Many early childhood education and services professionals recognize that they are most effective when they respond to the needs of the people they serve. Before you design and implement a collaborative action plan with a community group or community organization, you need to have a clear picture of the community's needs, the ways your program meets those needs, and the gaps between the two.

Ask Yourself

Most communities have multiple goals, issues, challenges, and visions. What do you want to accomplish in the communities you serve? What do you and your program want to address?

Does the community already have an action agenda you can support? Review existing community studies and community initiatives. What information and data are already out there? What does the data tell you? What does it *not* tell you? What will you do with the information?

When you try to address everything at once, you may end up burning out and not accomplishing anything. What do you believe are the most important issues or challenges facing your children's communities?

Coming together as equally involved partners is the only way you can collaborate successfully. Beware of the trap of efficiency! If you approach a community group or organization with your action agenda already set, you will create a power dynamic of leaders and followers that offers community members only the opportunity to follow you! You will build more trust and strengthen your program's relationship in the community when you find ways to connect with action agendas that are initiated from within the community. If you have done your homework by learning more about the community your program serves, you will have no problem determining what those initiatives could be.

What you think the children need may turn out to be very different from what they actually need. Say, for example, that a child in your program seems shy and withdrawn. Let's also say that this child speaks Somali at home. You may assume that you need to help her learn to interact more with her peers. If you were to visit her at home, however, you might see her engaged in active play with other Somali children and be surprised to find she is far from shy and withdrawn when she has the opportunity to interact with her peers in her own language.

Now, your goal might be to find ways to support this Somali child's process of assimilation, but in doing so, you will still need an active relationship with her community because your view of assimilation and her community's view of assimilation may be very different. Children of immigrant communities are often quickly assimilated into the dominant culture. Some adult members of their communities are saddened by the slow death of their native culture. They know their children will be good citizens, but will they be good members of their traditional cultural communities?

To determine what collaborative initiative, project, or action is most important to your children, families, and communities, consider the following questions:

- What do they need?
- What kind of initiative, project, or action will answer that need?
- Where should it be based?
- Who should be the spokesperson?
- What can your program do to help?
- How will the project respond to the unique needs and resources of the community?
- What do the community members want for their community?
- What do they want for their children?
- What do they want for themselves?
- What resources do they bring to the collaboration?

A needs assessment based on a community's resources, experts, history, needs, and goals for the future will give you an opportunity to create a partnership that can help a community forge its own path. Your program can participate in an authentic process of change and community growth, renewal, or sustainability. This is a leadership opportunity not to be missed!

EXERCISE

Collaboration, building relationships, networking, and recognizing the strengths or skills of others are important attributes of effective leaders.

- Think of a project or activity you would like to implement. If you could have five people on your planning committee, who would they be? These can be real or imaginary people, but for each one, think about the skills, expertise, and abilities each person brings to the team.

- What kind of citizen do you hope to grow through your program? What kind of community are you creating? What kind of society are you creating?

- How do you see your role in the balance between assimilating children into the dominant culture and keeping them as effective, productive members of their cultural communities?

- The strengths you see in young children in school and their skills, strengths, gifts, and opportunities that shine at home or in their communities can be very different. When and how do you observe children in environments other than your program? How can such observations assist you in helping children recognize and develop their own leadership abilities?

STRATEGIES AND FUNCTIONS

Leaders in collaborative community partnerships must use a number of strategies. The nature of such leadership requires that potential leaders develop a diverse set of skills and abilities to call on when different viewpoints, agendas, and interests compete for attention.

Most groups interested in community partnerships engage in many of the same functions. As you think about creating a partnership, you should consider who your constituents are, recruit members, arrange meetings, set goals, prepare strategies, consider forms of communication and publicity, and think about how to develop financial resources if necessary.

Take time in deciding what issue or challenge you want to address because this will determine which community leaders, community groups, or community organizations you want to recruit to your cause or project. Doing so will also determine whose attention you will try to attract through your action, cause, or project. Think in terms of constituents who rely on your program, audiences who should know about your program, and key players whose support and assistance you need.

Identifying constituents, audiences, and key players requires the core group or person to first develop clear goals. Asking these questions can help you achieve that clarity:

- What is the primary issue?

- What problems are involved?

- What are some possible solutions?

- What are possible ways to achieve the solution?

- What strengths and resources can your program and the community bring to the solution?

The answers to these questions must be determined early in the process. Although this question-and-answer process is part of strategizing, and a primary function of the core group or person will be to provide the information gathered to potential members. The focus here should be on what your program and you can do and how your leadership role will develop.

Once you have a group, focus on how to make it successful. Several conditions favor group success. First, the conditions in the community or the behavior of influential persons must be unsatisfactory enough to generate interest in change. Second, the group must have a vision of a more satisfactory state of affairs. Third, members must believe they will succeed. Finally, potential members must be tolerant of change, ambiguity, and innovation.

You are now ready to focus on a goal and the strategies and methods by which the goal will be achieved. In a guide for grassroots organizers, Si Kahn (1991) outlined seven indicators of a good strategy for achieving community action goals. I have added some examples to demonstrate how each might look. **Successful strategies**

Are thought out well in advance. Give yourself a time line that realistically takes into account how to include everyone.

Are built on people's experiences. Make use of the perspectives, skills, abilities, talents, and viewpoints team members bring to the group.

Involve people. Remember that all of your encounters with a community must be genuine and mutually beneficial; team members must be genuinely involved, and you must make sure everyone who needs to be involved is involved.

Are flexible. You are working with many people who have full lives, and few strategies proceed exactly as planned; be prepared to adjust your time line and focus with new alternatives and methods.

Have depth. Go as far as you can with your goal: Is there one more thing you can strive for or achieve? How about one more after that?

Are based on people's culture. Make sure the strategies and methods you have selected are based on the leadership styles and skills present in the cultures represented on your team.

Are educational. You and all those involved should gain valuable new knowledge from participating in community and social action—be intentional about what participants will gain from their increased leadership opportunities.

Another effective strategy for achieving community-partnership goals is to build coalitions of two or more groups. Coalitions have the advantage of increasing the potential resources of groups and demonstrating widespread interest in an issue or concern. What are some issues your program might share with the community you serve? Multicultural groups and multi-issue groups must pay particular attention to defining their coalitions' goals clearly, based on the groups' diverse interests. Such a coalition can provide a powerful means for meeting those goals.

Summary

In this chapter, we broadened the community-engagement work we began in chapter 4 by looking at leadership opportunities in programs serving young school children. Community leadership and collaboration provide abundant opportunities for ordinary people to become involved in extraordinary leadership activities. When the children in our communities have opportunities to witness adults as collaborative, effective, resourceful, and unified in their support of children, they may well be influenced by the roles and actions they see and may imitate the skills in the future. In chapter 6, you will have the opportunity to take a closer look at empowerment, followership, and advocacy. You will consider the kinds of environments that lead to empowerment and your role in creating them. In the section on followership, you will look at the other side of leadership—the strengths, skills, and responsibilities of followers. Then, you will bring empowerment and followership together and take another look at advocacy and its role in changing the early childhood education profession.

Story Time

Wei was the director of the after-school program in the community center. Most of the children who participated in the program were East African. For some time now, Wei had been thinking about the fact that the after-school program staff members had very few relationships with the East African community and even less knowledge about its history, needs, assets, and resources. The few times she had attempted to gather the parents and staff informally, she noticed that every conversation she overheard was based on the familiar roles of the staff and parent discussing the child in the context of the program.

Wei had recently read that when people have an opportunity to interact regularly in situations that take them out of their familiar roles, they begin to discover other shared interests and values and have more authentic conversations about a greater number of topics. A first step for Wei was to provide the staff opportunities to see the children outside the program. One of the parents told her about a community festival in which the children were going to perform a short skit and participate in a parade. Wei decided to work with the children to create invitations to the festival to give to the staff. Creating more complex relationships between the staff and the East African community would take some time, but Wei was excited. She had just received a copy of *Participatory Action Research Project Report* from the East African Child Care Task Force, and many of the action items for the community blended well with the program's mission and goals. Wei knew that attending the festival was just the beginning of what could be an influential, collaborative community partnership.

More Reading

Bailey, Paul. 1975. *Those kings and queens of old Hawaii: A mele to their memory.* Los Angeles: Westernlore Books.

Bruner, Charles, Karen Bell, Claire Brindis, Hedy Chang, and William Scarbrough. 1993. *Charting a course: Assessing a community's strengths and needs.* Falls Church, VA: National Center for Service Integration.

Child Care Information Exchange. 1999. *Inside child care: Trend report 2000.* Redmond, WA: Child Care Information Exchange.

Chrislip, David, and Carl Larson. 1994. *Collaborative leadership: How citizens and civic leaders can make a difference.* San Francisco: Jossey-Bass.

Dickinson, Tim. 2008. The machinery of hope. *Rolling Stone* Commemorative Edition, March 20, 60–69.

Dorfman, Diane. 1998. *Building partnerships workbook: Strengthening community education—The basis for sustainable community renewal.* Portland, OR: Northwest Regional Educational Laboratory.

Etzioni, Amitai. 1991. *A responsive society: Collected essays on guiding deliberate social change.* San Francisco: Jossey-Bass.

Ghiselin, Bernie. 1990. *Forging consensus: Building a dialogue among diverse leaders.* Special report. Greensboro, NC: Center for Creative Leadership.

Graham, John. 2005. *Stick your neck out: A street-smart guide to creating change in your community and beyond: Service as the path of a meaningful life.* San Francisco: Berrett-Koehler.

Greenleaf, Robert K., and Larry C. Spears. 2002. *Servant leadership: A journey into the nature of legitimate power and greatness.* 25th anniversary ed. New York: Paulist Press.

Kahn, Si. 1991. *Organizing: A guide for grassroots leaders.* Washington, DC: National Association of Social Workers.

Kindon, Sara Louise, Rachel Pain, and Mike Kesby, eds. 2007. *Participatory action research approaches and methods: Connecting people, participation, and place.* New York: Routledge.

Leary, Brent. 2008. Barack Obama's lesson in social media. *Black Enterprise*, June 18.

Life Magazine Editors. 2008. *The American journey of Barack Obama*. Boston: Little, Brown.

Lizza, Ryan. 2008. Battle plans: how Obama won. *New Yorker*, November 17, 46.

Maeroff, Gene I. 2006. *Building blocks: Making children successful in the early years of school*. New York: Palgrave Macmillan.

McCaleb, Sudia Paloma. 1997. *Building communities of learners: A collaboration among teachers, students, families, and communities*. Mahwah, NJ: Lawrence Erlbaum Associates.

McIntyre, Alice. 2007. *Participatory action research*. Los Angeles: Sage Publications.

Musson, Steve. 1994. *School-age care: Theory and practice*. Don Mills, Ontario: Addison-Wesley.

National Association of Elementary School Principals. 1993. *Standards for quality school-age child care*. Alexandria, VA: National Association of Elementary School Principals.

Sen, Rinku. 2003. *Stir it up: Lessons in community organizing and advocacy*. San Francisco: Jossey-Bass.

Silver, Nate. 2009. How Obama really won the election. *Esquire*, January 14.

Trawick-Smith, Jeffrey. 1997. *Early childhood development: A multicultural perspective*. Upper Saddle River, NJ: Prentice Hall.

T'Shaka, Oba. 1990. *The art of leadership*. Richmond, CA: Pan African Publications.

Wenner, Jann S. 2008. How Obama won. *Rolling Stone* Commemorative Edition, March 20, 128–31.

White, John. 1990. *Black leadership in America: From Booker T. Washington to Jesse Jackson*. 2nd ed. New York: Longman Publishing Group.

Zander, Alvin. 1990. *Effective social action by community groups*. San Francisco: Jossey-Bass.

Chapter 6

▲

Empowerment, Followership, and Advocacy

Empowerment is feeling, believing, and behaving as if you have power (in the sense of autonomy, authority, or control) over significant aspects of your life and work. Followership involves examining and reflecting on your responsibilities and influence as a follower and how these affect the leadership process and environment. In this chapter, you will have an opportunity to think more about what empowerment, followership, and advocacy mean for you as a leader in early childhood care and education. Understanding empowerment helps you find and use your words and actions in the leadership process. Understanding followership helps you decide on the kind of leader and leadership you choose to support.

In chapter 4, we looked at advocacy as a way to build bridges between our early childhood care and education settings and the communities we serve. In this chapter, we will look at advocacy from a different perspective: the perspective of speaking and acting from a place of empowerment and assuming the responsibility of followership. Understanding advocacy will help you combine your newly found internal empowerment with careful selection of leaders and leadership to exert more influence in local and national decisions that affect the early childhood education profession.

Empowerment

Many people today talk about being empowered—but what exactly does that mean? For most people, it means that we want to have more participation and more influence in what happens in our lives and our workplaces. We want work environments that not only support our participation and influence in making decisions and setting goals but ones that appreciate and expect our involvement as well.

Empowerment is speaking up, speaking out, advocating, and taking action on your own behalf. Empowerment is vital to the field of early childhood education, because the general public needs to hear from early childhood education teachers about the critical role we have in preparing the next generation. The public needs to hear about what can be done to increase the quality of the care and education children receive. These are especially important issues for women, who often have been socialized to react to change led by others rather than to become actively involved in the change process. As a teacher, you can begin studying, practicing, and reflecting on empowerment right in your own work environment among your coworkers and the parents and families of the children you serve.

Empowerment has been defined as the act of someone giving power or authority to someone else. Giving someone else power or authority implies that it can also be taken away again. For this reason, the best and strongest form of empowerment comes from inside—self-empowerment; it is difficult for someone to take away the power you find within yourself. Of course, this does not mean that leaders do not have a role in empowering others. Leaders create, support, and maintain work environments, processes, and policies that allow others to have some say and some control over what happens. This is what we mean by the term *supported empowerment*.

Empowerment can seem a lot like managing participatively, sharing resources or information, delegating responsibility, or enabling. Participative management is not the same as empowerment. Participative management is simply asking or allowing people to participate in the management process. Sharing resources or information can also be confused with empowerment. Sharing resources or information without sharing power is not going to result in people feeling, believing, and behaving as if they have control or influence over what happens at work. Delegating responsibility without sharing authority is simply passing on work to another person while keeping all the power yourself. Empowerment is not enabling. You enable a person when you support an environment and provide her with opportunities to stay the same way she is now. For example, suppose you have a coworker who is hesitant to voice her opinion. You would be enabling her if your solution is to voice her opinion for her. You would be supporting her empowerment if you decide to provide opportunities and space in conversations for her to speak and encourage others to listen to her.

SELF-EMPOWERMENT

Self-empowerment occurs when you decide to do something or say something to change a situation. You may be a person who has little trouble doing this, or you may be someone who has never really done anything like this before. Let's say you have a colleague who always seems to notice when the boys are misbehaving but not when the girls are. You really wish she would treat the children more equitably. Being empowered means you say something to her— even if you think her feelings may be hurt or she may get mad at you, even if you tend to be shy, and even if you are not her supervisor. Perhaps nobody told you that it was okay for you to talk with her or that you were expected to bring up troublesome issues with your coworkers. Nobody gave you the power or the authority to do that. You simply recognized that you had the power to address a difficult situation, and you did. That is self-empowerment. (It's also leadership!)

SUPPORTED EMPOWERMENT

Supported empowerment occurs when you and all of your colleagues work together intentionally to make sure that all of you have an opportunity to state what you want to happen. It occurs when you work together to make sure others value, hear, and respond to everyone else's perspectives.

Remember the coworker we discussed who seemed hesitant to voice her opinion? If speaking for her would be enabling, how can you support her empowerment to speak for herself? Supported empowerment means that you pay attention to her hesitation to speak up. You make space in conversations by asking her what she thinks. You encourage others to ask her opinion. You make sure you listen carefully to what she has to say, even if you do not agree.

Or consider the example of the coworker who was treating boys and girls differently. Perhaps you have a group agreement that teachers in your program will talk to one another about difficult issues and will raise their concerns about how the program is working. Perhaps you have a director who specifically asked you how your working relationships were going. When you tentatively voiced your concern about how boys and girls are treated differently by a particular coworker, she offered to help you think through how to approach your coworker, promised to debrief with you afterward, or offered to mediate if your concern became an open conflict. These are all examples of supported empowerment. You still have the power you always had to talk to your coworker, but the system and the people around you are supporting you to use that power. (And yes, you are still a leader in this situation!)

An Empowering Workplace

True empowerment is being intentional about ensuring that the work environment encourages and supports the full participation of all members. True empowerment is not just being able to say that everyone participated, you shared information or resources, you delegated responsibility, or you helped someone. You want to support empowerment because of the unique strengths and potential each person brings to the work experience. You want each person to develop into a strong and capable person. You want to hear what others think, believe, and want. You want the change that comes from shared power and influence because it lasts longer than change imposed by someone else. True empowerment means you want all of this for yourself—and it means you will create, support, and maintain an environment that provides it for others.

What does an empowering environment look like? What actions and processes would you see? Here are some things to look for:

- People freely share their opinions and perspectives.

- People openly seek out other opinions and perspectives.

- People really listen to each other and understand what the other person has to say.

- Lots of collaborating and sharing are visible; people do not feel the need to ration their energy or their resources.

- At meetings, lively conversation occurs, and everyone participates.

- Most decisions are made by the whole group, not by two or three individuals.

- People willingly participate in decision making because they know their opinions and perspectives matter to the rest of the group.

- Even when a few people do not agree with the decision that is made, they know that they didn't lose: their opinions are valued, and they are comfortable with the decision-making process, even when the decision is not one they would have made themselves.

- How people feel about things is evident to everyone; hiding feelings to protect oneself is uncommon.

- Even those people who tend to be shy or quiet are seen sharing their opinions and perspectives, and new people join in faster than they would in an non-empowering place.

ASK YOURSELF

Describe the ways your work environment empowers you. Are there ways your work environment seems to take power away?

In what ways do you share resources, information, and authority? In what ways does this empower you or others? Why does it empower you or others?

Empowerment does not mean you'll always get your way. There will still be times when things do not turn out the way you want. Being empowered does ensure, however, that you can do your best to make sure your needs and expectations are heard.

Empowerment is a shared leadership responsibility rather than the responsibility of a lone individual. It can happen only when each of us learns to collaborate, cooperate, and include all others. This is particularly important when considering collaboration and community leadership. When you have an opportunity to take an active role in how your work is designed and conducted, you will be more effective.

Your Role in Supporting Empowerment

As a leader in early childhood care and education, you can assist in the empowerment process in two ways. First, you can help create an environment that allows team members some control over their responsibilities and some confidence in their individual ability to create change. Second, you can examine your own feelings of control and self-confidence.

The first step is empowering yourself. When you are empowered, you become a model for others, and they can learn from your example. You can begin respectfully and firmly to increase the amount of influence and control you have at work with these steps:

- Tell others what you are feeling, thinking, and sensing.

- Clearly explain what you want, need, and expect.

- If an action or behavior conflicts with your personal values, say so.

- When someone speaks to you in an inappropriate manner, explain that you do not like to be treated that way.

- When you meet someone for the first time and he shortens your name (Debra to Debbie) or changes it (Juana to Jane), correct him.

If you have not had a lot of practice, empowering yourself will not be easy at first, but it will be very rewarding. I have never liked ethnic jokes, and when I was about twenty years old, I decided I would not let people tell them in my presence. It was very difficult at first, because people who were older than I tried to ignore my request, and people who were my age or younger would tease me and make fun of me. ("Close your tender ears, Debra! I'm about to tell an ethnic joke!") Sometimes I just left the room, and other times I stood my ground. Twenty-five years later, none of my friends and relatives tells ethnic jokes around me, and I'm no longer teased or ignored. Some of them probably do not tell such jokes at all because I ruined the fun for them. I felt good about standing my ground, and it worked.

Empowerment calls for new leaders—creative women and men who inspire others to go beyond simply carrying out tasks toward collaboration and consensus building. Empowering leaders must be compassionate, people oriented, and sensitive to the needs of diverse groups and individuals. They must be social architects who shape the work environment to support groups and individuals. As a teacher in early childhood care and education, you are a social architect already, because everything you do as a leader changes the people around you.

ASK YOURSELF

Describe how empowerment plays a role in your own personal experiences. Describe, for example, how you felt empowered or how you assisted in creating an empowering environment for others.

Followership

Despite all the discussions about leadership, few have addressed the ultimate test of effective leadership: is anyone following? Followers and the concept of followership have received increased attention lately in the study of leadership. Many of us may not reach the top levels of leadership in our workplaces or professions, but to identify who is a good leader, we must be able to fully recognize what makes leadership effective and become aware of how we develop those same qualities ourselves. All of us—teachers, assistants, aides, parents, trainers, and directors—must be able to recognize a good leader and resolve to follow only good leaders.

The word *follower* has negative connotations for those who think of followers as only passive and dependent. The idea of the passive follower fits well with the idea of the leader as the primary mover of history and change. In fact, no one leads all the time. A leader in one context is a follower in another. A good leader in one context is likely to make a good follower in a different one, because both require the same skills. For this reason, leaders are most effective when followers are also strong.

Author Robert Kelley explains why in his book *The Power of Followership* (1992):

- Leaders contribute an average of only twenty percent to the success of most groups.

- Followers are crucial to the remaining eighty percent of that success.

- Most people, regardless of title or salary, spend more time working as followers than as leaders.

Followership is a very responsible role. Followers risk empowering the leader, and followers must hold the leader accountable. In fact, followers often determine who is acceptable as a leader and if that leader will be effective. Followers show their leaders where to walk, and they validate the words leaders speak on their behalf. In essence, followers grant leadership to the leader.

ASK YOURSELF

What do you look for in a leader? What do you notice in effective leaders?

Followership is a serious responsibility. Choose a circumstance in which you would describe yourself as a follower. Describe the responsibilities you have in this role. For example, focus on your role as an employee, a voter, a daughter or son, a customer, or a client.

DIMENSIONS OF COURAGEOUS FOLLOWERSHIP

Ira Chaleff, the author of *The Courageous Follower: Standing Up to and for Our Leaders* (1995), identifies five dimensions of courageous followership:

The courage to assume responsibility. Effective and courageous followers understand that part of their role in the leadership process is to be responsible for whoever they allow to lead them, speak for them, and act on their behalf. If you find yourself following someone who is engaged in activities, actions, or behaviors that conflict with your expectations, needs, and values, you must decide what you intend to do about it and take responsibility for supporting such a leader.

The courage to serve. Effective followers understand the importance of service to others. Just as leaders need to serve their followers, courageous followers must serve their leaders. When you firmly believe in the vision, direction, and goals of a leader, you must support her and the leadership process through your words and actions. You must engage in activities and behaviors that help contribute to the group's ability to meet its goals or accomplish its mission.

The courage to challenge. Effective and courageous followers must challenge their leaders to attain a higher standard. If you notice that your leader is veering from the course set by the group, you have a responsibility to question the change and demand a response. Sometimes it is difficult to say, "I don't think that is what we had in mind." If you do not speak up, though, your inaction can be misinterpreted as consent or approval—whether you mean it to or not.

The courage to participate in transformation. Courageous followers know that change is hard, and they know that leaders cannot transform any workplace alone. Your actions, behaviors, attitudes, and expectations have just as much impact on your workplace as your director's or supervisor's. Effective followers understand that they are just as responsible as their leaders for how or if the workplace changes, so they participate actively and intentionally in the change process.

The courage to leave. Sometimes there simply is no way to reconcile your values with those of your leader. When this happens, courageous followers leave and seek an environment that more closely matches their values. This is often the hardest thing followers must do, especially when it means being unemployed for any length of time. There are alternatives, such as staying and being an unwilling supporter of something you do not believe in, or adjusting your own values to be more in line with your workplace's values. It takes courage to decide you must leave.

ASK YOURSELF

How would you describe yourself in terms of the five dimensions of courageous followership described above?

In what ways could you be a more courageous and effective follower?

The Interdependence between Leading and Following

The choice between leading and following is not an either/or situation. Leadership and followership are more like the ends of a continuum. Where we are on that continuum depends on the roles each of us plays and on the groups we are involved with. All of us have been, or will be, both followers and leaders. Followers often perform leaderlike acts and exhibit the same skills, styles, and abilities as good leaders. This does not necessarily mean that leaders must wait for followers to tell them what they want. Although followers like being treated with consideration and respect and appreciate opportunities to give input and to be creative, followers also expect leaders to provide clear direction, decision making, and authority when and where it is needed.

The relationship between leaders and followers is one of interdependence. Leaders never have as much control as the image of the all-powerful leader suggests, and followers are rarely as submissive as the stereotype of the passive follower suggests. Authority and responsibility for the leadership process belong to both leader and follower, and both need to develop new beliefs and expectations for their respective roles.

In the leadership process, leaders and followers depend on each other to meet their individual needs. Family child care settings, centers, and school-age care programs need children and families; politicians need voters; businesses need customers; social service agencies need clients; supervisors need workers; and religious organizations need members. Those of us who act in follower roles need the organizations we are a part of.

Effective followership is thoughtful, intentional, and should be taken seriously. What we do with our individual or collective power as followers determines what our leaders will do for us. Think about your workplace as an example. Yes, you may need your job as a teacher, and families may need safe, healthy, and educational play and learning environments for their children—but directors, supervisors, and family child care providers need you and the families as well. They need quality teachers and care providers if they want to maintain the quality of their programs. They need children to fill their programs. If either party is unhappy with the goals, values, attitudes, and actions of the other, the working relationships will fail, and someone will begin thinking about other options.

Effective followership plays a vital role in creating and carrying out your workplace vision. Groups and organizations that are on the cutting edge seek out independent, critical thinkers who have the courage to stand up for their ideas and beliefs. Providing an environment that supports effective followership means that the environment is also an empowering one. Unempowered people do not display the kind of followership we have been examining. Empowerment and followership must go hand in hand if the early childhood field is to take full advantage of the combined potential of its members. If you feel empowered enough to make your expectations and values known to your coworkers, you will feel empowered enough to make them known to your supervisor. If you feel empowered enough to make them known to your supervisor, you will begin to pay closer attention to your supervisor's leadership and whether or not it matches your expectations of a leader. If you are paying attention to your expectations of leaders and leadership, you will take your responsibility as a follower seriously. If this is true, you may well be ready to assume a bigger voice in a much larger conversation. You may well be ready for an expanded role as an early childhood care and education advocate.

Advocacy

Leadership in advocacy can be a matter of increasing your connections to families and communities as covered in chapter 4. Leadership in advocacy can also be a matter of broadening your circle of influence even further and gaining the ear of more and more people who make the decisions and choices for the early childhood care and education field. This will begin to happen naturally as your sense of empowerment and sense of followership grow: you will find yourself connecting with others who share your values, goals, and vision, and you will push, encourage, and support each other toward higher levels of action.

Like empowerment, advocacy must come from within. Only you can transform yourself into an advocate, because your role as an advocate can only be defined in terms of your actions—those steps you take to improve the lives of the children, their families, and those who serve them. When all of our individual efforts combine, we will begin to experience the difference a village can make in raising a child. There is a saying that you are only one drop in the ocean, only one tree in the forest, but without all those drops there can be no ocean, and without all those trees there can be no forest. In advocacy, never assume that someone else will do what needs doing and that your little piece of action won't matter. If too many people make this assumption, we will never get enough drops of water to make an ocean or enough trees to make a forest.

Most people who have changed the way we and others view our work did not set out to create a social or national movement. Most of them set out only to stick with some passionately held idea, value, or activity. One example is Maria Montessori, who did not intend to create an internationally known curriculum. She was only interested in accommodating a group of Italian children in need of something new and different in their learning environment. At the same time, she was an advocate for the children.

To be an advocate at this level is to take on the leadership role we discussed earlier in chapter 1, that of a spokesperson who carries forth the voices of those who might otherwise go unheard. This kind of advocacy is essential to the early childhood education field. We must continue to address recognition, professionalism, quality care and education, adequate resources, and the creation of coordinated programs that serve children and prepare them for kindergarten.

A good advocate is passionate and committed and believes strongly in her goal. A good advocate also knows deep down that it is possible to meet her goal. A good advocate will use many of the same leadership skills and abilities you have been examining throughout this book:

- Courage
- Effective communication and speaking skills
- Planning
- Vision
- Persistence
- Commitment

- Persuasion
- Clearly defined values

Do you have a goal, a vision, or an idea that you just know is not only possible but desperately needed? Have you asked others if they feel the same way? Whom have you talked to? What did they say? What could be some next steps for you?

In chapter 4, we considered a list of activities you could start as an advocate who builds bridges and links with families and communities. Here are some more suggestions about those first steps, along with some next steps to help you broaden your circle of influence and have more impact on the local and national decisions that affect early childhood care and education:

First step Start a parent teacher association (PTA) for your program if one has not been established.

Second step Arrange for your program's PTA to meet with the local elementary school's PTA.

First step Find out where various candidates stand on issues involving children, then vote responsibly.

Second step Work on the campaign team of a supportive candidate.

First step Tell parents, friends, and neighbors how you intend to vote and why.

Second step Ring doorbells for the candidate who supports your favorite early childhood education initiative.

First step If you are not ready to give testimony at a public hearing, support someone who is.

Second step Sign up to give testimony.

First step Always be prepared to explain what you do with children and why.

Second step Make an appointment to explain your work to your local senator or representative.

Summary

In this chapter, you had opportunities to think about empowerment, followership, and advocacy and what they mean for you as a leader. All three must come from within, and all three require you to think about your own power, control, actions, influence, and choices. When you are an empowered advocate who makes responsible followership choices, you take on a larger leadership role in advancing the goals and objectives of the early childhood education field.

Story Time

Veronica was in a tight spot. Her after-school program had just merged with another program, combining the staff and the children into one building. Veronica had been with the program for a year and enjoyed working with her team. At first, Veronica thought that combining the two programs was a great idea. She knew many of the other staff members, and many of the children knew each other because they lived in the same neighborhood. So why was Veronica uncomfortable?

As the weeks passed, Veronica noticed that the two sets of staff seemed to stay separate and were even beginning to say unkind things about each other. It reminded her of how kids on the playground behave: They were whispering in little groups and hoarding resources. They referred to the children as "my children" and "their children." She thought about saying something, but she usually kept to herself, and since she had not been with either program as long as some of the others, she wasn't sure it was her place to comment.

Veronica did not really like the new work environment—not for herself and certainly not for the children. She waited several more weeks for someone to do something or say something, but no one did. She didn't like the way she was being treated by the folks from the other after-school program, and she didn't like the way the staff from her original program wanted her to say bad things about the other team. She certainly didn't like the way the leaders, who were now codirectors, seemed unable or unwilling to talk about what was going on. Veronica could not see herself coming to work every day and being a part of all this much longer. She started looking for another job.

One day, one of the children came to Veronica and told her that a staff person from the other program always played favorites with her own kids and sided with them whenever the two groups of children had disagreements. That moved Veronica right out of her tight spot. It no longer mattered if her coworkers were really playing favorites or not—what mattered was that the children thought they were. Although Veronica had never been one to speak up or speak out, she knew she could not leave without advocating on behalf of these children, who were picking up on the unkind behavior the adults were modeling.

In good conscience, Veronica could not continue to follow the current poor leadership, and first she needed to let her coworkers and the codirectors know how she felt. The next time she felt pressured to join in disrespectful conversation, she offered a firm "No" and explained that she did not want to be a part of bad-mouthing the others. She also sought out individual members from the other team and tried to break down the communication walls. Finally, Veronica went to the two codirectors and explained to them she saw too much *us and them* in the after-school program and that it was unhealthy for the children. They both denied this could really be happening, but they said they would take a look at it.

Veronica did eventually leave. After she put her foot down, she felt awkward at work. Some people were afraid to talk to her, and others were just plain mad at her for pointing out their bad behavior. It was hard for Veronica, but she felt stronger than ever: she had taken a risk on behalf of herself and the children in the after-school program, and she had stood firm.

More Reading

Caldwell, Bettye. 2003. Advocacy is everybody's business. In *The art of leadership: Managing early childhood organizations*, rev. ed., eds. Bonnie Neugebauer and Roger Neugebauer, 46–48. Redmond, WA: Child Care Information Exchange.

Chaleff, Ira. 1995. *The courageous follower: Standing up to and for our leaders*. San Francisco: Berrett-Koehler.

Darder, Antonia. 1991. *Culture and power in the classroom: A critical foundation for bicultural education*. New York: Bergin and Garvey.

Federation of Child Care Centers of Alabama Staff. 1997. *More is caught than taught*. Montgomery, AL: Federation of Child Care Centers of Alabama.

Freire, Paulo. 1986. *Pedagogy of the oppressed*. New York: Continuum.

Graham, John. 2005. *Stick your neck out: A street-smart guide to creating change in your community and beyond: Service as the path of a meaningful life*. San Francisco: Berrett-Koehler.

Kelley, Robert. 1992. *The power of followership: How to create leaders people want to follow and followers who lead themselves*. New York: Doubleday.

Kostelnik, Marjorie. 2007. Modeling ethical behavior in the classroom. In *Child development: A beginnings workshop book*. Ed. Bonnie Neugebauer, 97–100. Redmond, WA: Child Care Information Exchange.

Sen, Rinku. 2003. *Stir it up: Lessons in community organizing and advocacy*. San Francisco: Jossey-Bass.

Wynn, Mychal. 2005. *Empowering African-American males: A guide to increasing Black male achievement*. Ed. Glenn Bascome. Marietta, GA: Rising Sun.

Zeece, Pauline Davey. 2003. Power lines: The use and abuse of power in child care programming. In *The art of leadership: Managing early childhood organizations*. Rev. ed. Eds. Bonnie Neugebauer and Roger Neugebauer, 25–29. Redmond, WA: Child Care Information Exchange.

Chapter 7

▲

Nurturing Leadership in Children

Throughout this book, we have looked at leadership from a variety of angles and perspectives. We have talked about what it means, what it does not mean, what it looks like, and what effects it has on others. We have seen many of the similarities between the characteristics and qualities of effective teachers and leaders; we have looked at how to be more intentional about translating teaching skill and ability into leadership skill and ability. We have explored ways to increase our relationships with family and connect with communities. Now it is time to transfer what we have learned to children.

In this chapter, you will have an opportunity to come full circle in your reflection on leadership development. It's time to look at how you can play an important role in teaching young children about leadership and leadership development. By thinking about leadership development as a lifelong process, you are putting yourself in a great position to help children identify their unique gifts and strengths, which are the foundation of their leadership skill and ability.

In the introduction, I noted that if children are present, they are learning. If you are present, you are teaching and learning. Become intentional about transferring the leadership aspects of the teaching and learning process. These ten topics will help you transfer what you have learned about leadership to supporting children's leadership development. Each topic includes a brief reminder of what was discussed earlier and some examples of what you can do with children:

Transference of ability (chapter 1). Transference is a skill you practice by applying your own abilities to new situations. Now you can assist children in doing the same.

Self-sufficiency and interdependence (chapter 1). This skill is important in discovering our own leadership potential. Interdependence helps us draw on each other's potential. Children need to learn when to do something themselves and when to get help from others.

Reflection (chapter 2). Reflection is the deep examination of what we do. Children will need to take baby steps in developing their reflective abilities.

Values (chapter 3). Values can be both personal and shared. Children begin developing and prioritizing their values from an early age. You can help them learn how different values interact.

Vision (chapter 3). Vision involves helping children to develop leadership skills, to transfer their natural imaginative skills to creating a vision, and to build strong communities.

Advocacy (chapters 4, 5, and 6). Advocacy is critical to leadership. You've learned what it takes to support others. Now it's time to teach children how to do the same.

Communication, social, and interpersonal skills (chapter 3). Early childhood is a critical time for children's social and emotional development and a critical time for your guidance in these areas.

Team building (chapter 4). Team building is part of children's social and emotional development, and you can play an important role in helping children understand the importance of working together effectively.

Empowerment (chapter 6). Children first learn about being empowered at age two. You can influence how they develop and grow from there.

Followership (chapter 6). We all can serve as both leaders and followers. Young children will face much peer pressure as they grow older. Learning to follow only good leaders will serve them well.

It's clear that children can benefit from being introduced to each of these topics, but how can you transfer these skills to them? We'll look at each topic in more detail, review what was discussed earlier, and examine three examples about children of different ages. Icons will indicate the ages of the children in each example:

- One for children between two and three years of age **2 to 3**

- One for children between three and five years of age **3 to 5**

- One for children between five and eight years of age **5 to 8**

Even though these are broad age ranges, keep in mind that all children develop at different rates in different areas. It is very important to provide children with activities that are age appropriate—age-appropriate reflection, visioning, team building, communication, advocacy, followership, and so on. Do not expect a two-year-old to be able to reflect in the same way as a five-year-old.

Transference of Ability

A major goal for this book has been for you to think of the many ways you can transfer leadership ability to different areas of your life. Many of the reflection questions were designed to encourage you to think about how to transfer your knowledge of child development to leadership skills in a number of situations and circumstances. We know that children transfer their play to learning possibilities—for example, when playing with blocks or playing grown-up. You can nurture children's leadership development by helping them think more about their skills and abilities and how to use them in a variety of areas.

2 to 3 A child begins to tell detailed stories, which means he is busily developing his communication skills. If the stories are about actual events, he is developing his ability to articulate what is going on. If the stories are made up, he is in the process of becoming a master storyteller or orator. Point out and encourage those skills. Let him know that many people who write books started out by doing what he is doing.

3 to 5 A child in your class often wants to play office and demonstrates quite a knack for organizing her playmates around specific tasks or roles. Support her organizing skills by letting her know that many work-places have office managers or directors who make sure all the work in the office gets done.

▲ **5 to 8** A child is successful in getting two of her friends to stop teasing one another. Let her know that some people call that skill *mediation* and that good mediators can help a group of friends continue playing together even when they don't always agree. Suggest that she try it with other children or with her siblings.

Self-Sufficiency and Interdependence

Effective leadership requires both self-sufficiency—knowing that you are a capable and competent person—and interdependence—finding ways to work together and making the best use of combined contributions. You can nurture children's leadership development by providing experiences that teach them the difference between self-sufficiency and interdependence and that demonstrate the need for both skills in leadership.

▲ **2 to 3** Some tasks may require self-sufficiency. A child masters the task of making his own lunch without any help. Comment on the fact that he is becoming very good at paying attention to his needs and taking care of himself.

▲ **3 to 5** You observe a child making a block city all by herself. She is quite efficient, so her city is large. You notice that all of her buildings are similar. You've seen another child make many different buildings. The next time it is appropriate, create an opportunity for them to work together. Later, you can ask the first child to compare what she liked about making a city alone with what she liked about making one with her friend.

▲ **5 to 8** Some tasks require interdependence. A group of children decide that the gerbil's cage needs to be cleaned. As they figure out which person should hold the gerbil, which person should put new flooring down, and which person should carry water, let them know that they are learning how to use what each person is good at to get the job done.

Reflection

Reflection is taking a look at yourself and what you are doing by remembering and thinking about past experiences and what they mean. In the leadership process, reflecting on your experiences gives you the opportunity to analyze your leadership skills and abilities and decide if the results are what you really intended. You can nurture children's leadership development by making sure they have the same opportunities. Remember that reflecting on an experience often develops leadership more than the experience itself.

2 to 3 A child gets into trouble for hitting. Ask her what happened, why she thinks it happened, what the consequences were, if the results were what she intended, and what could she do differently next time.

3 to 5 Children develop reflection skills when they have opportunities to talk and think about their work, play, and actions. When you start your day with the children, ask each one to say, draw, or show what they would like to learn during the next activity. Then have the children proceed with the activity. After the activity, have each child say, draw, or show what they think about what they did.

5 to 8 Give children opportunities to reflect on the experiences of others. During a story, a child tells you that he thinks a character should do something differently. Ask him what he would do in the situation, why he would do it that way, and how the ending would be different if the character had done what he recommended.

Values

Learning about leadership requires you to think about your beliefs, principles, and ideals. Your values determine how you will achieve your vision—what steps or actions you will take. Children's values are still in the developing stages (like ours), and you can nurture their leadership development by helping them understand how they can apply what is important to them when making decisions.

2to3   Give children lots of opportunities to make choices and think about the choices they make. When a child wants to do two different activities but only has time for one, let her know that she must choose. When she makes her decision, ask her why she made that choice. Explain to her that she is deciding what is most important to her.

3to5   Let the children make their own list of rules for the class. Have them each come up with their own rules and then narrow the rules down to the few that everyone agrees are important. Explain to them that they are creating shared values for each other and themselves.

5to8   Make a list of values, such as truth, caring, listening, and fairness (for ideas, see chapter 3). Ask each child to pick the two values he thinks are most important and have him explain why he feels that way. Have each child give an example of a time when he used that value.

Vision

Having a vision means conceiving of a better place, situation, or circumstance in the future. Your vision is what you see as a better future, and you will use your values to determine how to achieve that vision. Children are often remarkably good at envisioning. They imagine, pretend, and fantasize quite easily. You can nurture children's leadership development by arranging specific and intentional opportunities for them to imagine, pretend, and fantasize.

2to3   Two children are arguing over what to do during an activity. Explain to them that they will have another chance to work together the next day, and ask them to talk about what they will do differently the next day so that they have fun together.

3to5   Make up a story for children that stops in the middle and presents a problem. Ask each child to make up a happy ending for the story. Have the children draw pictures, sing a song, tell a friend, act out the ending, or express themselves as they choose. Explain to them how each child created a different ending, a different vision of a better future for the story.

▲ **5 to 8** Give each child an opportunity to use possibility thinking by letting them play *What if?* For example, ask the children the following questions: What if you could have any pet you wanted? What if you had a hundred dollars? What if you lived on the moon? What if you were the boss of Disneyland?

Advocacy

Leadership in advocacy involves collaborating, speaking up, and taking action. Advocates decide how they feel about something, share their knowledge with others, and think of what they can do about it. You can nurture children's leadership development by giving them opportunities to think about what is important to them, how to involve others, and what actions they can take.

▲ **2 to 3** Some children may become concerned about a little puppy or other animal in a story you are reading. They wonder what can be done even though it is only a story. Ask them for ideas about what they would do for the puppy if they were in the story. Then write down or have them draw pictures of their ideas.

▲ **3 to 5** Ask children to talk about the environment and the things people do to harm it, such as littering. Have each child come up with a different way she can help—for example, by carrying a plastic bag in her coat pocket to put wrappers in. As a group, discuss how the children's combined efforts can make a difference.

▲ **5 to 8** During the holiday season, many organizations hold canned-food drives or coat drives. Ask the children in your care to think about what they would like to do to help. Have them choose another group to work with, such as the local elementary school, and decide how they would like to contact the group.

Communication, Social, and Interpersonal Skills

Leadership involves communicating and getting along with people. Often leadership potential is first recognized through verbal skills and social interactions. Strong verbal skills are often indicative of strong organizational skills and an ability to rally others. Strong social skills are often indicative of an ability to collaborate with many different groups. Strong interpersonal skills often demonstrate an ability to interact with others and really understand their perspective. You can nurture children's leadership development by helping them understand and practice different skills and reflect upon their usefulness.

2 to 3 You tell a group of children that you are going to read a story about the trees and the sun. One child reminds you that yesterday you said you were going to read a story about a fish and a crab. Let her know that she was using good listening skills and that listening and paying attention are important when people talk with each other.

3 to 5 One little girl in your program likes to play with both girls and boys, but the other girls don't like it when she plays with the boys. She has explained to the girls that some of the boys are her friends, but that hasn't helped. Let the little girl know it is okay to have more than one group of friends and tell her you notice that she seems to get along with lots of children.

5 to 8 A child in your group likes to practice using new words, some of which are not age appropriate. Encourage the child's emerging verbal skills by helping him choose two new words to learn every week; help him think about ways to use the words throughout the week. Explain that many important people, such as President Barack Obama, use lots of different words and that he is going to be able to use a lot of words himself by the time he leaves your program.

Team Building

Team building happens when you create processes, interactions, and activities that bring all of the people in your group together and use each person's gifts and strengths to achieve a common goal or vision. You can nurture children's leadership development by making sure they have opportunities to think specifically about what a team is and why they may need one.

Team-building activities may be especially important for girls, who may not have as many opportunities as boys to play team sports.

2 to 3 A child wants you to ask two other children to help her make a tower out of blocks. You ask her why she chose these specific children, and she tells you that one of them is a really good block carrier and the other always has good ideas about how to make the tower taller. Tell her she is using good team-building skills by thinking about what each child is good at and by knowing how each child might help her make a block tower.

3 to 5 When three or more children are involved in dramatic or pretend play involving a doctor's office, pay attention to the roles they choose, such as doctor, parent, baby, or nurse. Explain to the children that they have put together a very good team because a good team is made up of people who have different skills. Ask them what other roles they might want on their team the next time they play.

5 to 8 Help children begin to think about each other's strengths and abilities. Encourage them to describe what each group member is good at doing. Be sure to remind them that everyone is good at something. Make a list of strengths and abilities, and ask the group for ideas about things they can do as a team of talented children.

Empowerment

Empowerment is feeling and believing that you have adequate participation, control, and influence over what happens in your life and behaving accordingly. When you feel empowered, you begin to speak up, speak out, advocate, and take action on your own behalf. You can nurture children's leadership development by giving them opportunities to solve problems and disagreements on their own so they can begin to feel capable and confident in their ability to make a difference. You can also help them understand the difference between being empowered and controlling others.

2 to 3 Make sure free time is structured into your daily program so children have the opportunity to choose their own activities. Some children have days that are entirely scheduled by adults, which allows no time for activities of their own choosing. You can allow for choices as simple as choosing between drawing, painting, or coloring, or as complex as choosing from a variety of workstations.

▲3to5 One little boy in your program constantly picks up his baby sister and carries her to wherever he is playing. At the beginning of the year, she doesn't seem to mind, but after a few months, you notice that she is trying to squirm out of his grasp. Let him know that she is getting older and wants to make her own choices about where to go. Encourage him to call to her when he wants to play with her; tell him she will come if she's interested.

▲5to8 One boy in your program is becoming very annoyed because another child always bumps into him whenever she passes by. He doesn't do or say anything because he hopes she will eventually stop. You can encourage his sense of empowerment by having him explain to the girl that he does not like being bumped and wants her to stop.

Followership

An effective follower is very selective and intentional about whom he accepts as a leader and decides if that leader will be effective in achieving a goal or vision that is meaningful to him. Everyone has been or will be a leader and a follower. You can nurture children's leadership development by helping them begin to understand the importance of the follower's role and by helping them to learn to take turns being leader and follower.

▲2to3 A child tells you she is upset because another child is making her pull all the other children in the wagon. When you ask her if she wants to continue pulling the wagon, she says "No." Have the girl explain to you why she feels she has to do what the other child says. Ask her to think about what would happen if she said no to the other child. Ask her what would happen if she continued to pull the wagon even when she didn't want to.

▲3to5 In your classroom, one child is in charge of setting up snack, and each day he can choose another child to help him. One day he chooses a child who has helped many times before, and another girl notices. She tells him it would be more fair if he gave all the children a chance to help. Let the girl know that by speaking up she is helping the boy become a better snack leader.

▲ 5to8 You notice that one child regularly asks other children if she can join their group to play. Within a very few minutes of joining, however, she converts their play into something she has chosen. Let her know you notice that she changes the other children's play into her own game, and ask her why she doesn't play what they are playing. Tell her how important it is to learn to play the games that other children start so she can learn many more games besides her own. Explain that good players can play other people's games as well as their own.

It is important to recognize the leadership talent in children, to prepare them for more challenging leadership experiences, and to help them develop into the next generation of leaders. As a nurturer of leadership development, you can prepare children to be leaders in their communities and society at large by providing them with appropriate opportunities to learn more about leadership and the strengths and abilities they have.

We already understand the importance of affirming all that is good about individual children. Affirming what children do right can help them develop a sense of worth and purpose. When you validate the many areas in which children demonstrate leadership ability, they will be encouraged to explore their own potential and recognize their many strengths and gifts. Of course, this does not mean that you should not discuss areas that need improvement. Children need feedback not only about their strengths but their weaknesses as well. They need to recognize those leadership skills at which they excel and those leadership skills that need to be strengthened.

ASK YOURSELF

> **Think about each child in your center, home, program, or classroom. Which leadership skills and abilities do you see blossoming? How can you help a child build on or enhance each skill or ability? What about each child's leadership**

challenges? How can you help each child address or sup-
plement her leadership challenges?

We all know that children are more likely to imitate adults
than to do what adults tell them, so always remember that
the children in your presence are watching and imitating
you. What do children learn about leadership from you
when they watch you interacting with other children and
other adults? As you grow more intentional in your own
leadership development, you can begin to focus on how to
model appropriate leadership behavior for children.

What are the three most important things you look for in a
leader? How do you model those for children?

Summary

In this chapter, we followed the old proverb that says we should lift as we
climb by examining how we can help children develop, understand, and
strengthen their own leadership ability. We examined ten topics covered in
earlier parts of this book, each of which included examples of how to think
about children's developmental stages and how to use each skill. Effective
leadership produces more leadership and more leaders. When you transfer
what you have learned about your own leadership development to helping
children learn about theirs, you are truly learning to lead!

You have reached the end of this book but not the end of your journey. In
many ways, your journey is just beginning. You have been introduced to many
ways of looking at and thinking about leadership and your role in the leadership process. Leadership takes place in a variety of forms and contexts and
on a variety of levels. Continue on your reflective journey by continuing to
think about what leadership means to you and about who you are as a leader.
Every time you interact with another person, you have an opportunity to
bring leadership to life through interdependence, service, respect for cultural
variations, interpersonal communication, empowerment, and advocacy.

Remember that leadership is developmental. Take your time and be patient with your own learning. Take extra care of the leaders and followers around you and also the leader in you. You can only get better and better. We need your leadership! The children, their families, and the field of early childhood care and education need what you have to offer. Every lifelong journey begins with a single step. I think you are well on your way!

STORY TIME

This story was inspired by a true story about my daughter, Siobhan.

Debra had been running a small early childhood care and education program in her home for almost a year. She felt fortunate to be able to do this because it allowed her to stay with her sons, Aaron and Porter, and to be home when her second-grader, Siobhan, came home from school. In the evenings, Debra had been reading a book about leadership development for early childhood educators and was reflecting on her own leadership development. She had been trying out new activities every day and was really beginning to see her own growth. One day, after she had just finished reading the last chapter of the book, she was talking with one of the parents while Siobhan sat playing with her subtraction flash cards. Debra was explaining to the parent how she was planning to attend a rally on Saturday to advocate for better wages in early childhood care while her husband and her mother-in-law took the children to a neighborhood festival. Siobhan piped right up: "Mom, I thought you said Grandma was in Olympia this weekend." Debra was surprised. It had not even occurred to her that Siobhan might be listening; she seemed to be very involved with the flash cards. Caught off guard, she ignored Siobhan and finished her conversation.

That evening, Debra thought about her mixed feelings and what she would do. She was annoyed that Siobhan was listening in on her conversation, but she also knew that the ability to listen, remember, and pay attention were important skills for children to develop. Debra also thought about the amount of time Siobhan spent in her presence and wondered what other things she might be learning and absorbing when Debra was interacting with other adults. Finally, Debra wasn't sure if she admired the confidence and self-esteem that made Siobhan comfortable in joining an adult conversation or if she was concerned that her daughter was beginning to join adult conversations more often.

The next day after the rally, Debra decided to think very intentionally about Siobhan's leadership development and how she could use it as a springboard for thinking about the leadership development of the other three children in her care. What kind of leader would each child be twenty years from now, and how could Debra help nurture that leadership? She made a list of each child's gifts and strengths and thought very carefully about what it would look like to have the children exercise these. For example, while she did want Siobhan to grow in her confidence and understand increasingly complex language, she also wanted her to understand that she should not join adults' conversations if she was not invited to and that she did not always have to repeat what she heard.

Most of all, Debra reflected on what it felt like to have children watching her, listening to her, and imitating her all the time, whether she liked it or not, whether she noticed it or not. She wondered what other things children may have heard her say or seen her do when she didn't realize it. Debra understood for the first time what it was like to model appropriate leadership behavior for her own and other people's children. She knew it was a big responsibility, but she asked herself, "When was the last time you were involved in the lives of children and it *wasn't* a big responsibility?"

More Reading

Chen, Jie-Qi, Mara Krechevsky, and Julie Viens. 1998. *Building on children's strengths: The experience of project spectrum.* New York: Teachers College Press.

Elkind, David. 2007. *The power of play: How spontaneous, imaginative activities lead to happier, healthier children.* Cambridge, MA: Da Capo Press.

Gottman, John M., and Joan DeClaire. 1998. *Raising an emotionally intelligent child: The heart of parenting.* New York: Simon and Schuster.

Federation of Child Care Centers of Alabama Staff. 1997. *More is caught than taught.* Montgomery, AL: Federation of Child Care Centers of Alabama.

Helm, Judy Harris, and Lilian Katz. 2001. *Young investigators: The project approach in the early years.* New York: Teachers College Press.

Jalongo, Mary Renck. 2008. *Learning to listen, listening to learn: Building essential skills in young children.* Washington, DC: National Association for the Education of Young Children.

Kostelnik, Marjorie. 2007. Modeling ethical behavior in the classroom. In *Child development: A beginnings workshop book.* Ed. Bonnie Neugebauer, 97–100. Redmond, WA: Child Care Information Exchange.

Lewis, Barbara A. 1991. *The kid's guide to social action: How to solve social problems you choose and turn creative thinking into positive action.* Ed. Pamela Espeland. Minneapolis: Free Spirit Publishing.

McCaleb, Sudia Paloma. 1997. *Building communities of learners: A collaboration among teachers, students, families, and communities.* Mahwah, NJ: Lawrence Erlbaum Associates.

Trawick-Smith, Jeffrey. 1997. *Early childhood development: A multicultural perspective.* Upper Saddle River, NJ: Prentice Hall.

Young, James C. 2006. *From roots to wings: Successful parenting African American style.* Chicago: African American Images.

Index

community forums, 93
community influences on communication, 54
community knowledge, 77–78
community leadership, and social action, 87–90
community needs, 29
community partnerships, collaborative, 97
community partnerships, goals for, 98–99
community relationship opportunities, 93–94
community spaces, 93
competencies, development of, 19–20
competencies, for ECE teachers and leaders, 38–39
competition, as cultural value, 55
confidence, and leadership development, 31–33
constructivism, 17
cosponsored programs, 86
creativity in leadership, 40
cultural context of leadership, 51–53
cultural differences, 30, 54–55
cultural diversity, 52–53, 53–55
culture and cultures
  and community vs. individual needs, 29
  competition vs. collaboration in, 55
  and conception of leadership, 7
  of the family, 29–31
curriculum, emergent, 16

D

decision-making processes, collaboration in, 75–76
different perspectives, 43, 51–52
directive style of leadership, 14–15
disposition, in ECE teacher and leader competencies, 39
diversity
  cultural, 52–53, 53–55
  in ECE, 51, 56
  in values, 60

E

early childhood care and education (ECE)
  as continuous process, 2
  diversity in, 51, 56
  obstacles to leadership development in, 3
  teacher and leader competencies, 39
emergent curriculum, 16
empowerment
  of children, 127–128
  community collaborations and, 90–91
  defined, 103–105
  and followership, 113

leaders and, 6, 108–109
  and leadership development, 120
  as power used with someone, 9
  as shared leadership responsibility, 107–108
  in the workplace, 106–107
enablement, empowerment vs., 105
Erikson Institute, 72
European American families, 29
exercise in collaboration, 96
exercise in reflection, 46–47
extrinsic motivation, 44–45

F

facilitation, 9
facilitative style of leadership, 14, 15–16
familiarity, in leadership opportunities, 41
families
  culture of, and leadership development, 29–31
  expectations in, and leadership characteristics, 31–33
  low-income, oldest girls in, 27
  parallels between workplace and, 34–35
  size of, and leadership development, 28
family development knowledge, 39
family leadership styles, 35–37
fantasizing, and vision, 124–125
fiscal management and planning, 39
flexibility in leadership, 40
followership
  in children, 128–129
  courageous, 110–112, 111
  defined, 103
  effective, 112–113
  and empowerment, 113
  and leadership, 109–110
  and leadership development, 120
followership-leadership continuum, 112–113
future orientation, as attribute of sound vision, 61

G

genuine encounters, 91–92
Ghiselin, Bernie, 94
gifted classes, 19
girls, and team-building activities, 127
girls, oldest in low-income families, 27
Greensboro One Task Force, 94

H

hands-off style of leadership, 35–37
human development, and leadership development, 16–21